The Lensball Photography Handbook

The Ultimate Guide to Mastering Refraction Photography and Creating Stunning Images

Marvin Lei

rockynook

The Lensball Photography Handbook
The Ultimate Guide to Mastering Refraction Photography and Creating Stunning Images
Marvin Lei

Project editor: Jocelyn Howell
Project manager: Lisa Brazieal
Marketing coordinator: Katie Walker
Layout and type: Gary Hespenheide
Cover design: Aren Straiger

ISBN: 978-1-68198-578-7
1st Edition (1st printing, February 2022)
©2022 Marvin Lei
All images © Marvin Lei unless otherwise noted

Rocky Nook Inc.
1010 B Street, Suite 350
San Rafael, CA 94901
USA

www.rockynook.com

Distributed in the UK and Europe by Publishers Group UK
Distributed in the US and all other territories by Ingram Publisher Services

Library of Congress Control Number: 2021935014

All rights reserved. No part of the material protected by this copyright notice may be reproduced or utilized in any form, electronic or mechanical, including photocopying, recording, or by any information storage and retrieval system, without written permission of the publisher.

Many of the designations in this book used by manufacturers and sellers to distinguish their products are claimed as trademarks of their respective companies. Where those designations appear in this book, and Rocky Nook was aware of a trademark claim, the designations have been printed in caps or initial caps. All product names and services identified throughout this book are used in editorial fashion only and for the benefit of such companies with no intention of infringement of the trademark. They are not intended to convey endorsement or other affiliation with this book.

While reasonable care has been exercised in the preparation of this book, the publisher and author assume no responsibility for errors or omissions, or for damages resulting from the use of the information contained herein or from the use of the discs or programs that may accompany it.

This book is printed on acid-free paper.
Printed in Korea

Contents

Acknowledgments

I just wanted to first off take this time to thank my family and close friends for supporting my passion in photography over the years. For helping me come up with new ideas and having the patience to watch me test them. Especially through the instances of me losing my lensball to the ocean or standing with me knee-deep in a swamp to capture a sunset. I would also like to thank my supporters for motivating me to continue capturing my visions and providing me feedback on my work. Last but not least, thank you, Nicole, for always being an inspiration to my work and even sticking around after enduring my encyclopedia of Dad jokes.

About the Author

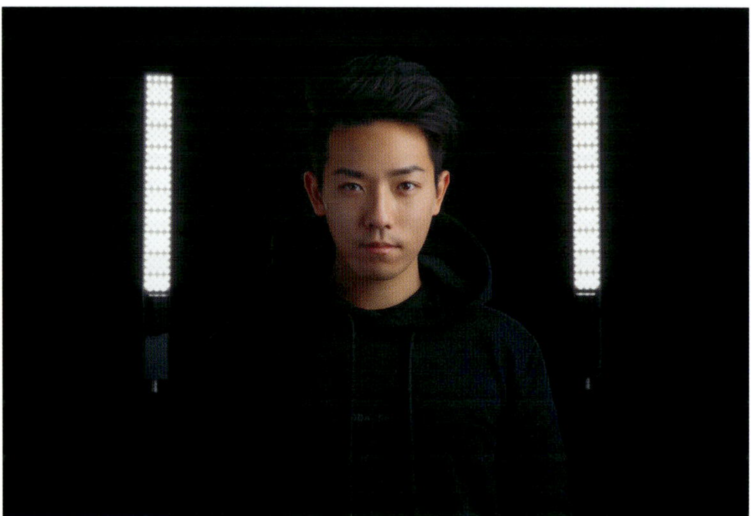

Marvin Lei is a photographer and digital artist based on Long Island, New York, who focuses on evoking sentiments through his work. Graduating from Stony Brook University with an MBA and Engineering degree, he spent much of his free time as the President of the University's Photography Association, educating students on the key elements in image-capturing as well as post-processing. Passionate in his technical field, he often challenges himself with experimental props and unconventional perspectives.

Introduction

My name is Marvin Lei and I am a photographer and digital artist. I specialize in portraiture and lensball photography and have been practicing my art for the past ten years. I began shooting with lensball in 2017 and was fond of how creative you could get with the photos. I decided to challenge myself and took at least one image in every environment I shot in. There was a lot of trial and error, but the experience helped build my understanding of the final picture. In the past few years, I began hosting local portrait photo walks and editing tutorial sessions to help photographers in my area become more accustomed to capturing subjects and posing models. During this period, I also brought the lensball on location as a prop and it garnered a good amount of interest. Over time, I accumulated more and more questions on my methods of shooting and editing, which served as a foundation for this guide.

In this guide, I will cover how I shoot and the settings I use for all my lensball images. Quick disclosure: there is no right or wrong way to shoot with a lensball, or to shoot any photo for that matter. The images you capture are your art and you should follow what you believe makes a picture interesting or beautiful. I am just here to provide you with guidelines and hopefully inspire you to develop your own style. For the sake of this guide, I explored both nature and urban landscapes to illustrate the different techniques and lighting styles that can be used in these scenarios. I left some of the images unedited so you can see what I look for in an image before I post-process it. The original composition and the lighting make up the majority of the image. Most of my photos are taken at 24mm, 35mm, 50mm, and 70mm, as those are the most common focal lengths for photographers. This will also help you visualize which lens configuration would be the most helpful for a specific location or environment.

The topics covered in this book were garnered from my years of trial and error. These concepts are geared toward photographers who have a general understanding of photography and who also have an interest in exploring the different avenues to shooting with lensball. Even if you have many years of experience, you may find some tips helpful that you can bring to the table on your next shoot.

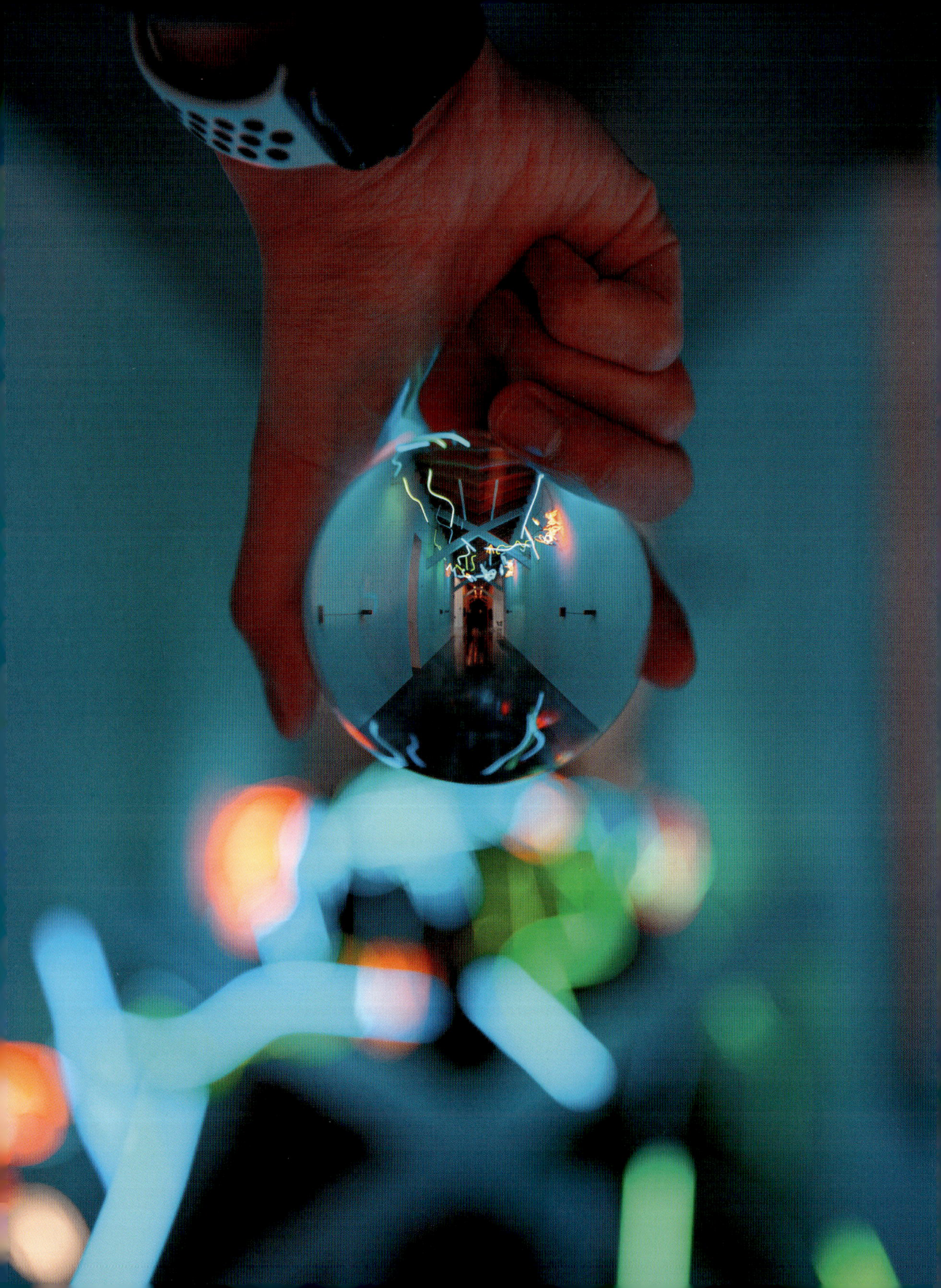

CHAPTER 1

Physics and Properties

If you find yourself struggling with a creative block or want to experiment with something new, try taking a lensball with you the next time you go out to shoot. I've seen a lot of people create amazing work with this tool, and in turn, it has changed the way I shoot and compose my images. Unlike any ordinary prop, the lensball has some key elements that make it very unique.

First, the lensball has very similar properties to a wide-angle lens. Placing the ball too close to a subject will provide a fish-eye look, whereas moving it away from a backdrop allows it to encapsulate a large canvas. Straight lines will appear curved the farther they are from the center of the crystal ball, an effect also known as *barrel distortion* (figure 1.1). Many photographers utilize this attribute to create a strong perspective on the center of the image as well as to keep all of the scene in sharp focus.

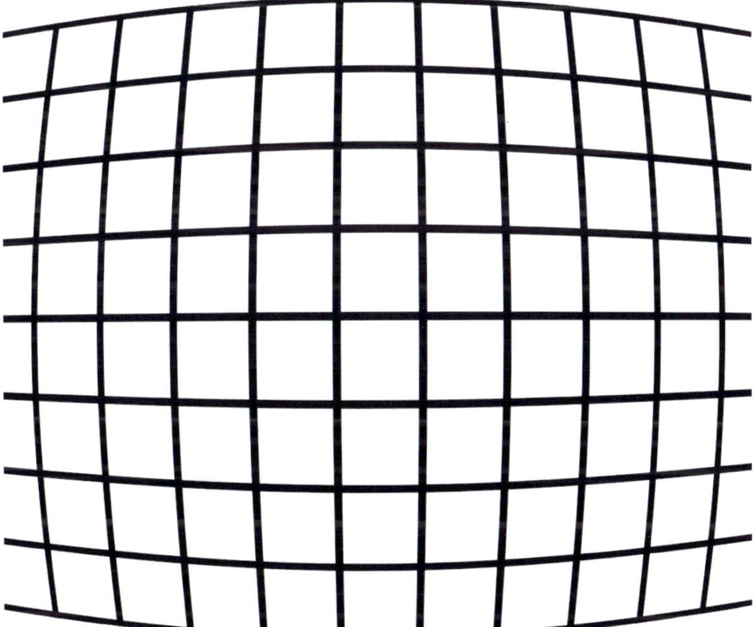

Figure 1.1
Barrel distortion can be visualized as straight parallel lines in the center of the image that curve outward as they move closer to the edges. This property places more emphasis on the middle of the composition. Barrell distortion commonly occurs with the use of wide-angle lenses and can be easily rectified in post-production with Lens Correction settings.

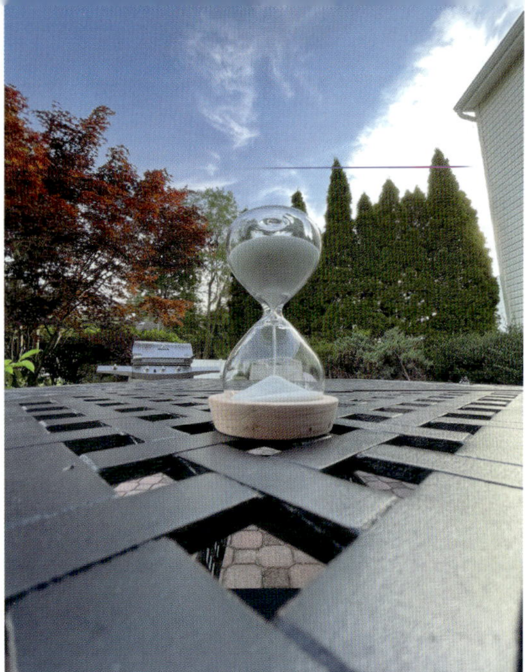

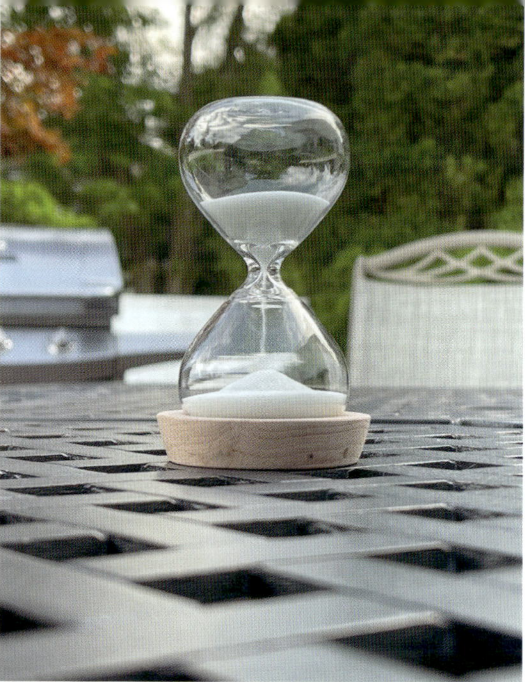

Figure 1.2a

This image shows an example of wide-angle distortion, which can emphasize the subject by warping its surroundings. Everything in the image (foreground and background) appears to be in focus. This phenomenon is known as the *pan focus* effect, and it is widely used by landscape photographers to capture a scene with a single focus.

Figure 1.2b

On the other hand, telephoto lenses produce what's called *selective focus*. This is generally great for portraiture, as it separates the subject from the background.

Second, the lensball exhibits what some people know as *refraction*, meaning that when light passes through a medium with different density, it bends and provides a distorted image to the viewer. This effect is typically exemplified when you're trying to grab an object in a swimming pool or looking at someone through a glass of water. However, the curved surface of the sphere redirects these light rays toward a focal point, which then flips, creating an inverted image at a certain distance (figure 1.3). This type of lens is also referred to as a convex lens. If you've ever removed your lens from your camera, you've seen this exact effect.

One thing to note is that since this converges light into a single point, you will need to be cautious when using a lensball in harsh, direct sunlight. You are basically holding a large magnifying glass, but your hand is the surface. I generally avoid shooting it handheld during midday, as you can feel an occasional sting if you hold it up against the

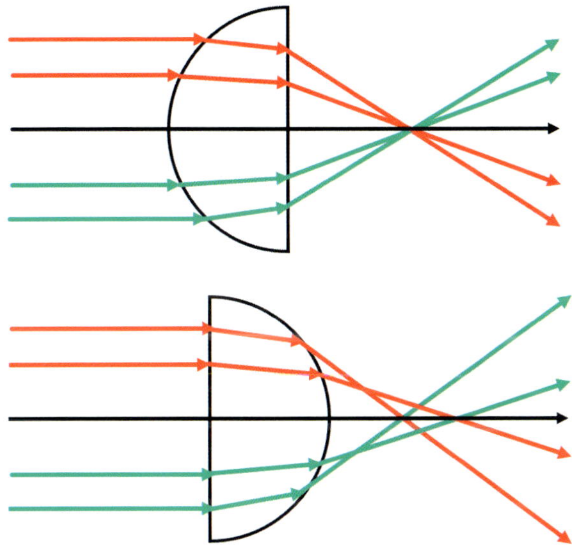

sun for too long. This is one of the reasons you see psychics keep their crystal balls in a curtained room—otherwise, if left exposed to the sun, they wouldn't have a location in which to operate their business.

The lensball is really just a bi-convex lens, which, in simpler terms, is a really thick magnifying glass. In physics, a bi-convex lens has the same curvature on both sides of the lens (figure 1.5). Since the lensball is a sphere, the opposite sides will always have the same radius of curvature. This explains why images are projected upside down and wrapped around the ball.

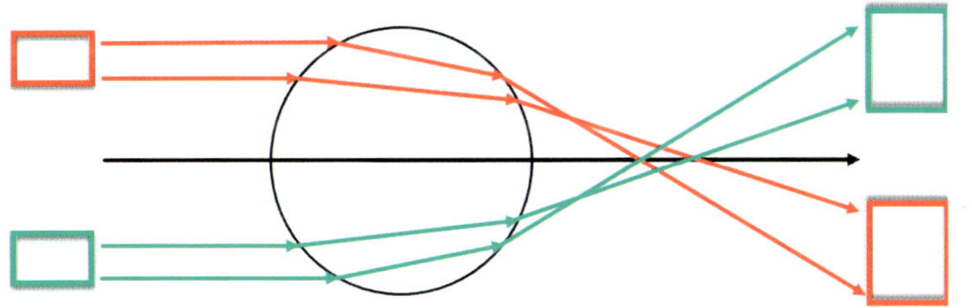

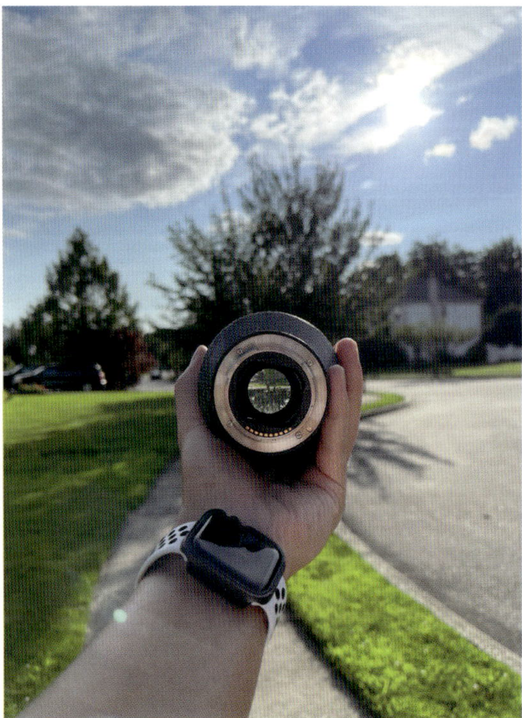

Figure 1.6

A camera lens follows the same principle where the image is flipped past a certain focal point. It is also made up of many different lens elements to produce a sharp image for the camera sensor. Things like chromatic aberration and spherical aberration are also corrected in this configuration.

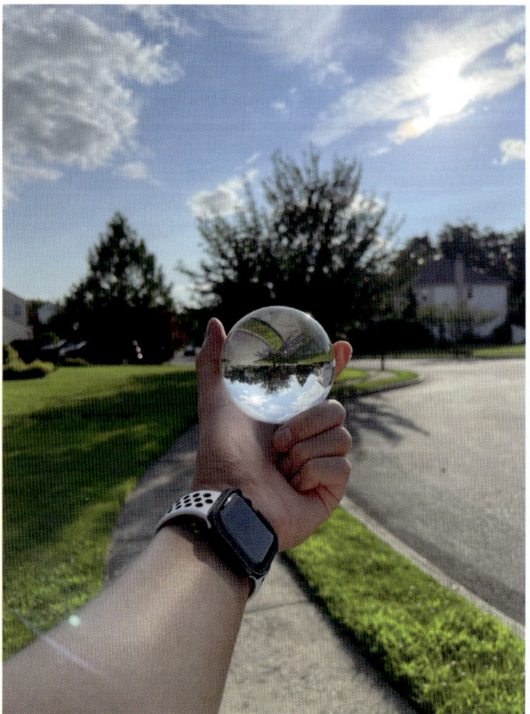

Figure 1.7

The lensball exhibits noticeable warping near the edges while the image in the center looks relatively flat. Later in this book, you will see many compositions that work well with this distortion.

Essentially, shooting with a lensball gives you the opportunity to capture two different images within the same frame: a mirrored wide-angle composition and telephoto composition. If this is your first time using one, I suggest you bring it out with you and familiarize yourself with how your shooting location appears within the ball. Bring it to a beach, a park, or the city and observe how certain elevations and surfaces drastically affect the overall image. The more you shoot with it, the better you will understand its characteristics, allowing you to plan future shoots before you even make the trip.

CHAPTER 2

Camera Settings

One of the key elements to creating the perfect image is utilizing the appropriate camera settings for your vision. I won't go too deep into explaining how to balance the exposure triangle, but there is some basic knowledge all photographers need to keep in mind during a shoot: aperture, shutter speed, and ISO. I capture most of my images in manual mode and configure the settings in the order mentioned. While it is not necessary to shoot in manual to photograph a lensball, it will save some headache to nail the shot.

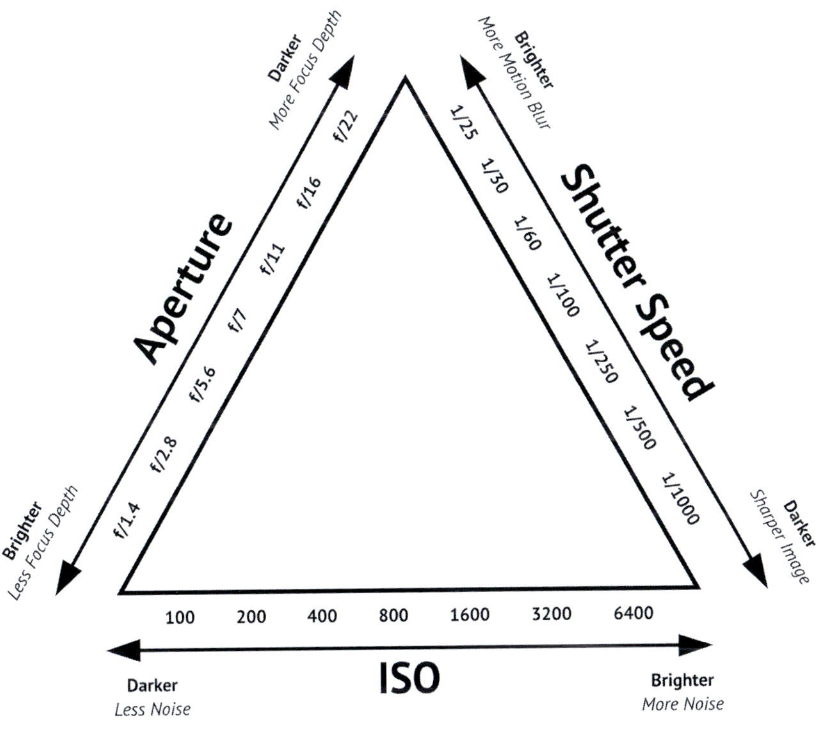

Figure 2.1
Visualizing the exposure triangle can help you achieve the correct combination of settings for your desired exposure given your lighting situation. The three values (aperture, shutter speed, and ISO) are dependent on one another, so be mindful of how changing one will affect the values of the other two.

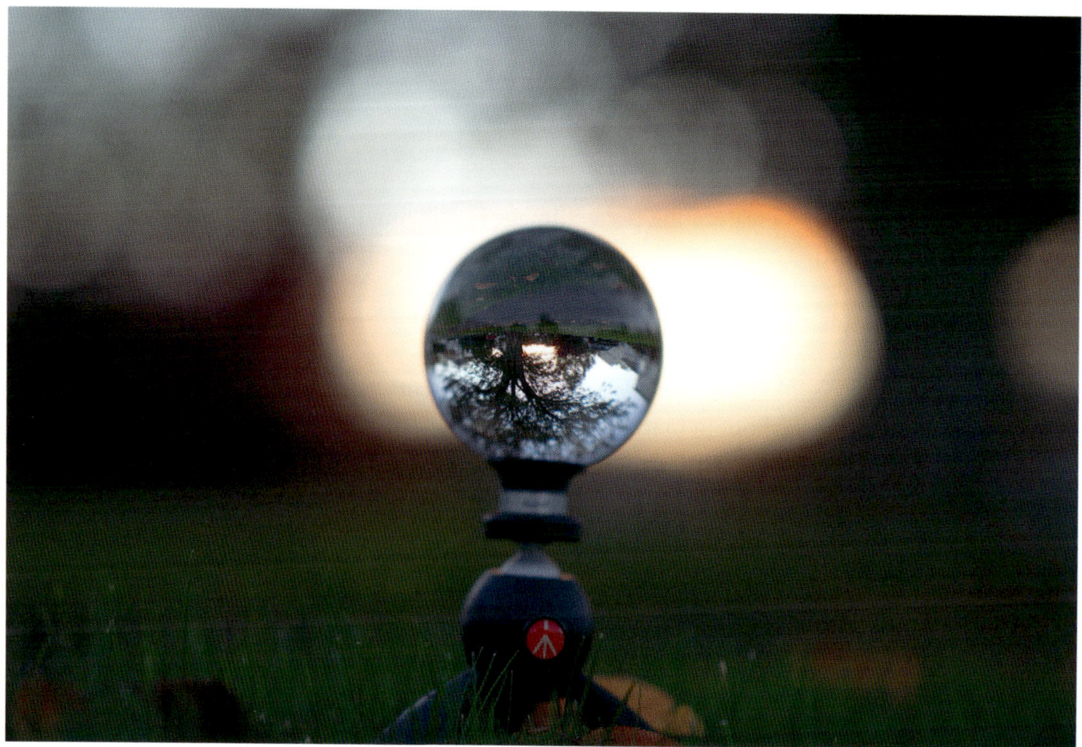

Figure 2.2a

85mm | f/1.4 | 1/200s | ISO 100

Too wide of an aperture can cause you to lose detail in the overall image. I would recommend setting the aperture to a focus depth that encapsulates at least 90% of the lensball. In this figure, only the center of the image is sharp.

Aperture

The aperture number, or f-stop, dictates the size of the lens opening, which in turns controls the amount of light hitting the camera sensor. The value works inversely with how much light gets through: the smaller the number, the larger the opening, and the larger the number, the smaller the opening. Aperture also affects the depth of field, where setting a low f-stop would capture a thin plane of focus and vice versa. I generally shoot at a very wide aperture to create separation between the lensball and the background. I recommend not going below an aperture of f/2.8, as the edges of the ball become too blurry and your image gets less defined. The goal when shooting a lensball is to get the center of the ball tack sharp while leaving the rest of the image more abstract. When dropping apertures to values like f/1.4, you run the risk of losing definition of the sphere, leading to an image that looks out of focus overall (figure 2.2a).

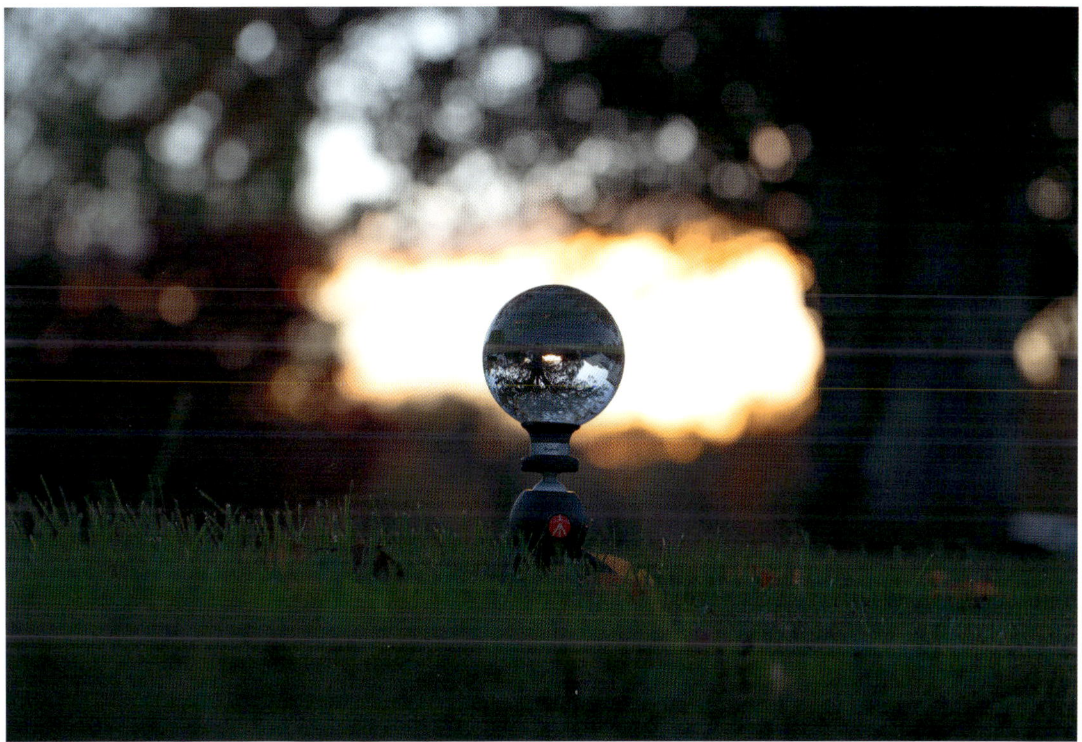

Generally, the highest aperture value I use for lensball shots is f/5.6. Depending on the focal length of the lens and the distance to the ball, it can still maintain a strong separation between the foreground and background. If set up correctly, you can acquire a very sharp-looking shot with smooth bokeh. The aperture should be the first thing you set, as it will determine the overall feel for the image. This is one of the settings that cannot be easily altered in post-processing. Another thing to understand is that increasing the aperture too much will lead to darker images because there will be less light hitting the sensor. To compensate for this, you can make adjustments to the shutter speed.

Figure 2.2b
100mm | f/5.0 | 1/200s | ISO 250

Shutter Speed

After setting the aperture, the next step is to set the shutter speed, which determines the amount of time the sensor is exposed to light. Depending on the environment, I typically expose my photos between

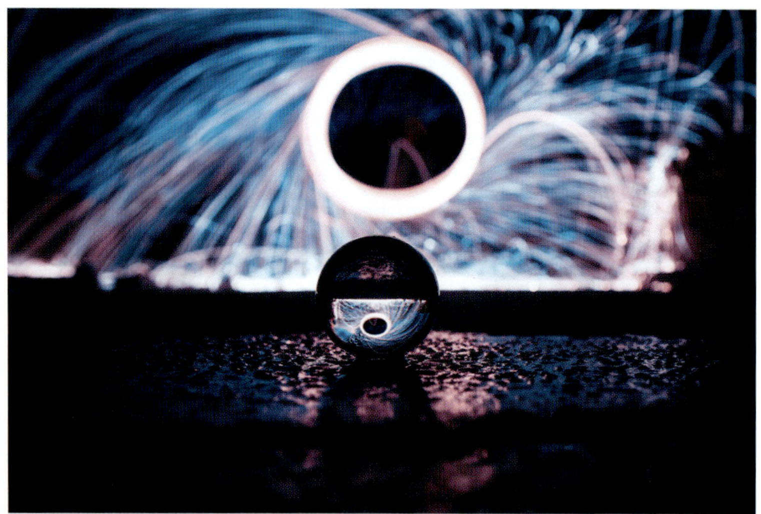

This image illustrates the effect of using a long shutter speed of 6 seconds to capture a long-exposure shot of lit steel wool spun at night. The camera was placed a few inches away on the ground, with the focus manually adjusted for a clear shot of the inside of the ball. Shooting with a long exposure allowed me to keep my ISO at a minimum to reduce noise and preserve as much detail as I could.

+1 and −1 stop of light. Relying solely on metering is not always enough to obtain the best exposure. I recommend viewing your histogram when setting up the composition to confirm the highlights are not blown out and the shadows aren't too dark. These details may be unrecoverable when you go to edit the image later on. If you are unsure, you can always shoot the same shot with three separate exposures and decide later what details are necessary for the final product.

In terms of setting shutter speed, I generally abide by the golden rule to keep the shutter speed no slower than 1/(the focal length). This is to ensure you do not get blurry images when shooting handheld. For example, if you are shooting at 50mm, your shutter speed should not dip below 1/50th of a second—e.g., you don't want to use 1/40, 1/30, etc. I would even go as far as keeping it to 1/(2x the focal length), just to play it safe. There are times when using slower shutter speeds can help enhance your photos. A prime example is utilizing a tripod or stable surface to capture light trails or steel wool through a lensball.

ISO

Adjusting the ISO value should always be the last step of configuring your manual settings. This is only necessary when your images are too underexposed and need to be brightened up. The caveat here is that setting too high of an ISO will lead to unwanted noise in your image, which can be a pain to edit out. Basically, you are pushing your camera sensor to capture more light, which can introduce speckles on the image from the increased electrical charge. This is the reason I set my ISO last, as it is only meant to boost up the exposure when the other two settings are maxed out for the capture.

However, there are still alternatives to reduce grain in your photos when editing them. Astrophotographers use a technique called image stacking to help reduce noise by combining multiple captures and removing the random pixels that do not belong. But for our purposes I would just recommend shooting in a well-lit environment to maintain a comfortable ISO. Nowadays, most full-frame cameras can handle up to 1600 ISO fairly well without registering much noise. For my shoots, I try to keep the ISO between 100 and 400, and will max out at 1600 if shooting handheld indoors.

Autofocus Points

Things get tricky if you do not have the appropriate autofocusing configuration when shooting lensball photos. Leaving this decision to your camera's discretion can give you a frustrating experience when attempting to nail sharp focus for your shot. I've seen a number of lensball photo submissions where the camera recognized the glare on

Figure 2.4

24mm | f/2.8 | 20s | ISO 4000

This image was shot at 4000 ISO, which introduced a good amount of noise into the image. Astrophotographers tend to shoot with higher sensitivity to bring out the details in the night sky. Luckily for them, noise blends well with stars. However, each camera performs differently with light sensitivity. There are camera bodies that are created to perform well in low-light situations at the expense of image resolution.

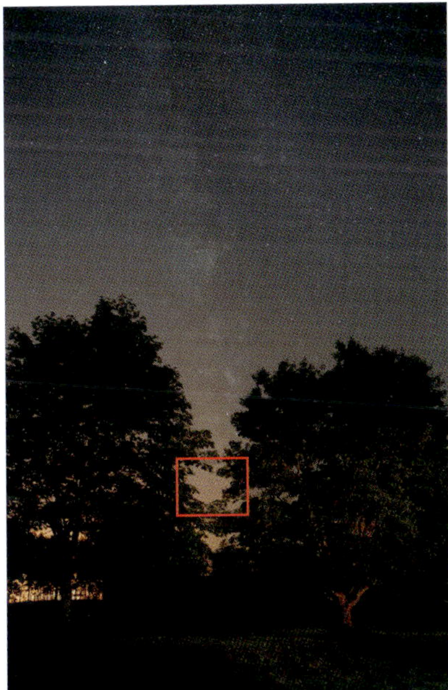

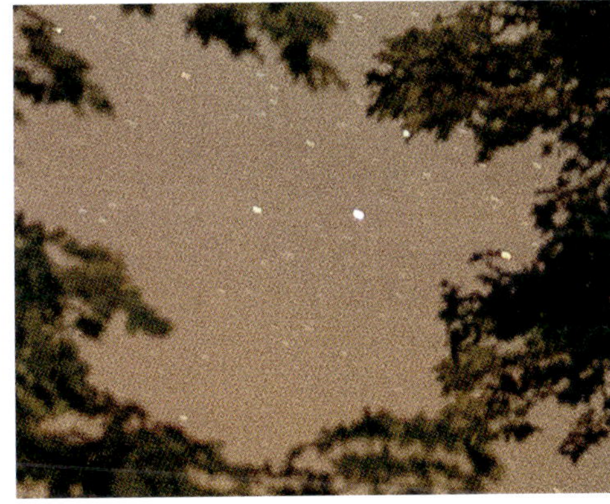

the front surface as being in focus and left everything else blurry. This can occur if you use the Dynamic Area AutoFocus or 3D Tracking settings.

If you want more control over the focus area, I recommend shooting with Single Point AF so the camera will focus within a small user-designated area. This gives you the control to pinpoint exactly what part of the frame you want to be the sharpest, which in this case would be the center image within the ball. You will have eliminated all the "guessing" that the camera would have to do to choose between multiple autofocusing points.

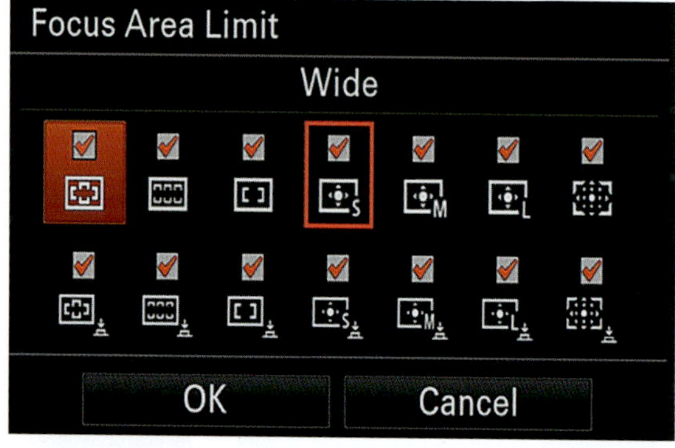

Figure 2.5
This is an example of the focus-area selection screen for a Sony mirrorless camera. Many cameras will have this adjustment in their menu settings.

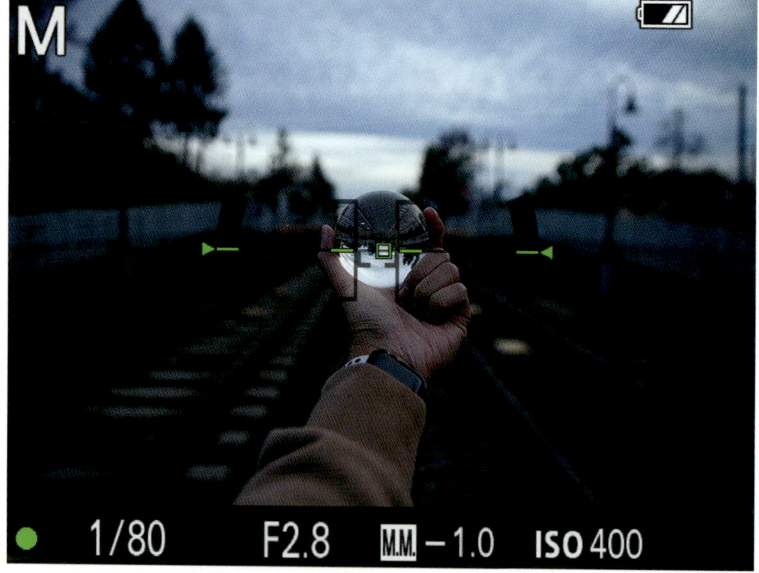

Figure 2.6
Selecting the smallest focus area will allow you to have pin-point accuracy in controlling what part of the lensball you want the camera to focus on. For example, in this capture I have aligned the focus point where the train tracks meet the horizon. Your camera acquires focus the quickest in high-contrast areas. You may notice some delay or "travel" when trying to focus on indis-tinguishable objects like the bushes and the dirt.

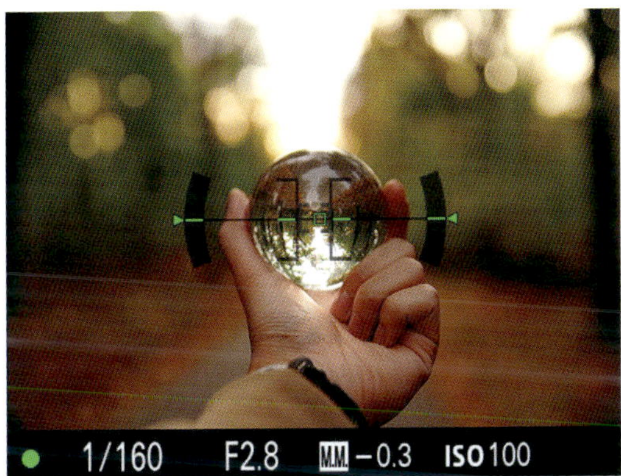

Figure 2.7a
This shows an in-camera view of what I find important when capturing a photo. Pay attention to keeping your minimum shutter speed in line with the exposure, as well as maintaining a balanced composition.

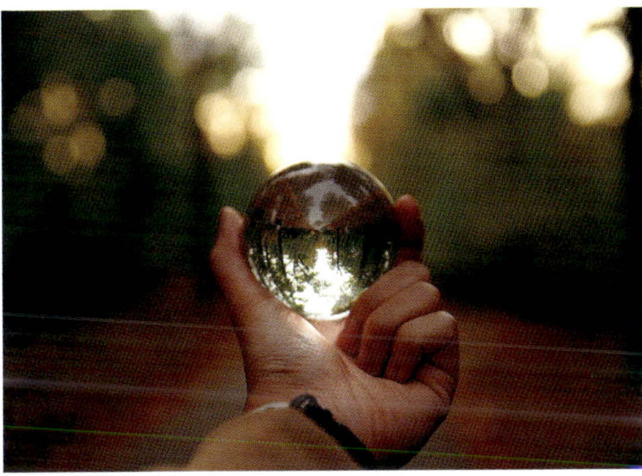

Figure 2.7b
Selecting a focus point in the center of the ball rather than at the edge allows the blur to naturally transition into the middle. It guides the viewer's attention toward the main subject of the frame, which in this case is the intersection of the leading lines where the path and treeline meet. This is primarily an artistic recommendation, but it doesn't hurt to try this out.

I also use Single Point AF to assist in setting up my composition. By anchoring the focusing point on, let's say, the center of the frame, I will know to press the shutter button when the lensball lines up with that square. This prevents any wavering, which may cause the image to lean too heavily on one side or the other. Because you are shooting for "two compositions," having this setup will make the composition process significantly easier. In my workflow, I use the smallest AF point my camera allows and move it over the point of highest contrast within the center of the ball. This guarantees that I get my "subject" in focus every time without accidentally focusing on the front or side curvature of the sphere.

AF-S versus AF-C

Continuing on this topic, let's discuss the appropriate times to choose between using Single shot and Continuous focus servo modes (these setting names may differ depending on camera manufacturers). This is not to be confused with Single Point and Dynamic Area autofocusing, which were mentioned earlier. These focusing modes determine how your camera behaves when you press down on the trigger.

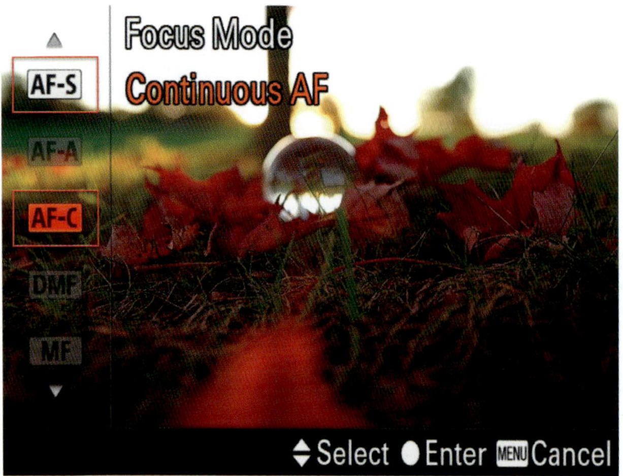

Figure 2.8

Tip: I generally use Continuous autofocus when shooting handheld, and reserve Single shot AF for when I'm using a tripod or stationary platform. Any slight movement can throw off the focus from the time you half-press the shutter button to the moment you release it.

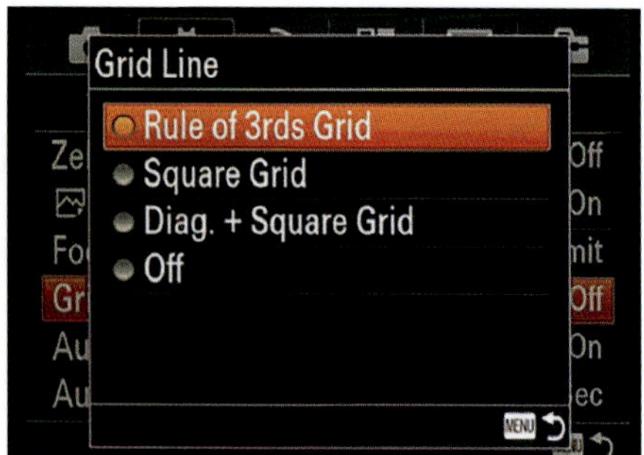

Figure 2.9

I enable the viewfinder grid lines display and horizontal leveler to help compose the shot. Cameras generally come with a number of compositional overlays to help photographers balance their images. Since most cameras have small screens and viewfinders, displaying these guides will save you the process of cropping or rotating your photos later. Although it is not a law to follow the rule of thirds or leading lines, it will help make the overall image more interesting and guide the viewer's eyes toward the subject.

Single shot autofocus (AF-S) basically locks the focus the moment you half-press the shutter button and keeps it locked until you release or execute the shot. This is excellent when the lensball is kept at a set distance away from the camera. The only downfall is that if you move forward or backward, your focusing plane will move as well. This should be reserved for shooting with a tripod or if you are confident in remaining motionless while lining up the shot. In a handheld situation, I like to set the camera to high-speed burst mode and Single shot AF and shoot three images per focus lock. This way if I do sway or move the focusing plane, I will likely get one image in perfect focus.

An alternative would be to use Continuous autofocus; however, this may pose a problem depending on the lens and camera body you use. Some telephoto lenses will "hunt" to focus by zooming back and forth until the lens finds a high-contrast area to lock onto. This may work for wider compositions, but in my experience, it has caused me to miss focus a number of times.

CHAPTER 3

Looking for Lenses

How to choose a lens is probably the thing I'm asked about the most when it comes to lensball photography, and it is also the most debated subject depending on your style and end goal for the image.

Before we dive into this topic, you will need to know whether your camera has a cropped or full-frame sensor. Your compositions may require different focal lengths depending on your sensor size. For example, if a crop-sensor camera has a crop factor of, say, 1.6x, a 50mm lens will act more like an 80mm lens. It is notable that having a larger sensor will produce better images, but the best sensor size for you is really dependent on what your photography goals are.

Crop-sensor cameras are lightweight and compact, along with their lens selection. These setups are great for those who are on a budget and are capturing photos primarily as a hobby. Full-frame bodies contain sensors that match the common size of 35mm film. These cameras will require more expensive glass and are a prime choice for most professional photographers. There are also medium-format cameras, which have an even larger sensor for studio use and can cost a few thousand dollars for just the body alone. Image quality is really high, but at the cost of large file sizes. I shot all the content for this book with a full-frame mirrorless camera, so all the lenses I mention are true to size.

The topic of lenses can be split up into two categories: prime versus zoom, and wide versus telephoto. As a recap, prime lenses have a fixed focal length and are known to be sharper, faster, and more lightweight than zoom lenses. However, zoom lenses offer more versatility to change the focal length, which makes them ideal for on-the-go shooting. Wide versus telephoto simply differentiates lenses with focal lengths less than or greater than 50mm, respectively.

As a portrait photographer, you will find me sporting telephoto prime lenses on a majority of my shoots, primarily because they help me capture sharp images with a lot of compression. And just as likely, you will see a lot of landscape or real-estate photographers mounting

Figure 3.1a

[50mm | f/2.8 | 1/1250s | ISO 100]
This illustrates the amount of real estate lost from an image when using a crop-sensor camera. It essentially crops the image from a 50mm view to an 80mm view. This may seem like a lot of space, but it can be compensated for by using wider-angle lenses to expand the frame. There are, however, other issues that come with smaller sensors, such as a decrease in image quality and low-light performance. For the sake of this book, we will focus primarily on the properties of a full-frame camera.

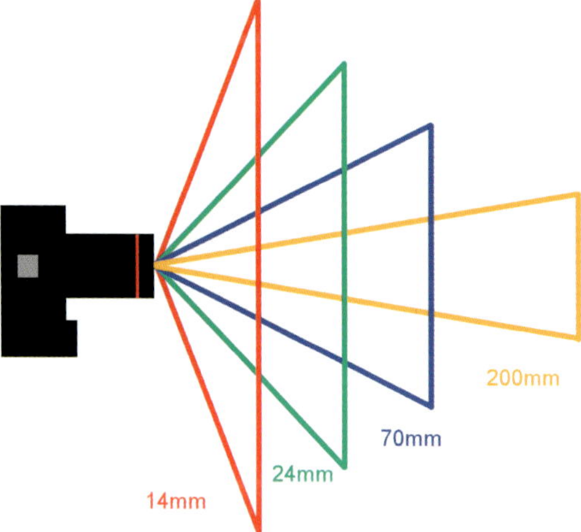

Figure 3.1b
This diagram shows how different angles of view work with your scenery. A 14mm focal length will work great for capturing an entire scene, while a 200mm focal length will tighten the frame and make the subject appear closer.

wide zoom lenses on their cameras because they frequently shoot in different locations and need to capture more of the environment. However, for lensball shots, you can use either practice interchangeably. Due to the sphere's unique wide distortion, you can use a range of focal lengths to capture the same scenes and produce amazingly different results. The question you want to ask yourself here is if you mind carrying multiple lenses with you to produce very sharp images. Or, on the other hand, you may prefer to travel lightweight with one lens and do not mind the difference in image quality. One additional consideration to keep in mind is that prime lenses have the ability to use wide apertures like f/1.2 to f/1.8; however, as previously stated, wide apertures are not practical for getting a sharp lensball image.

For the following examples, I took pictures of the lensball at common focal lengths to demonstrate how the framing and background compression looks. All photos were captured at each lens's lowest aperture.

14mm

This is typically the widest full-frame lens most photographers will have in their arsenal. With the ability to capture a viewing angle of around 115 degrees, this lens is an excellent choice if you're trying to envelop an entire scene with one shot. As mentioned earlier in regard to the shutter speed and focal length relationship, the 14mm focal length will allow you to capture better shots in low-light conditions, as motion blur may not be much of an issue. Many astrophotographers take advantage of this property to capture long exposures of the Milky Way without introducing star trails from the Earth's rotation.

Although this lens does sound versatile, it may defeat the purpose of using a lensball as the subject. The background of the image may overpower the details within the lensball due to the distortion of an ultra-wide-angle lens. The end product will look more like a fish-eye view of the landscape with a glass sphere interrupting the composition.

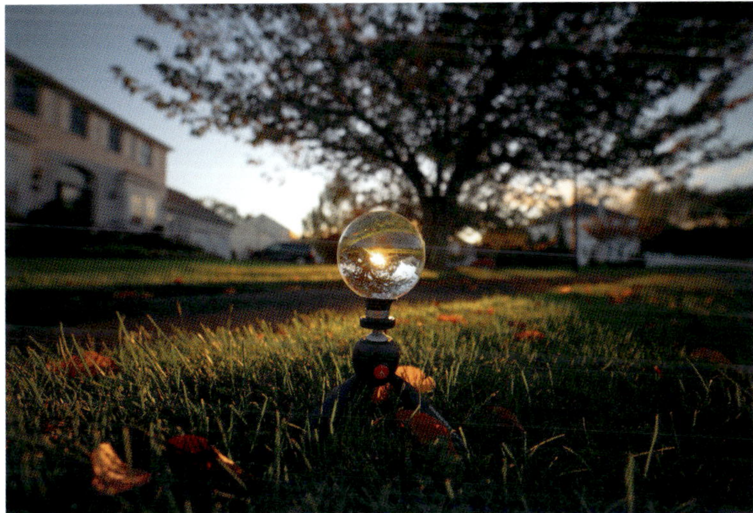

Figure 3.2
14mm | f/2.8 | 1/250s | ISO 100

Don't get me wrong, there are many unique setups that can incorporate a 14mm lens into their photography workflow, but it may not be feasible for everyday lensball photography.

24mm

The 24mm pancake lens is what most photographers recognize as their first prime landscape lens. Similar to 14mm, this focal length is excellent for capturing landscapes as well as interior spaces. It is wide enough to provide a grand view of your surroundings, but still provides emphasis on your subject. Because of how close you will need to be positioned to a subject, this focal length is generally not desirable for portrait photography due to the wide-angle distortion and lack of separation between subject and background. It is advisable to have a lens that includes this focal length if you wish to encompass more of the background in your lensball photography. You will be able to capture a sharp focus on the ball while creating a subtle blur with the backdrop.

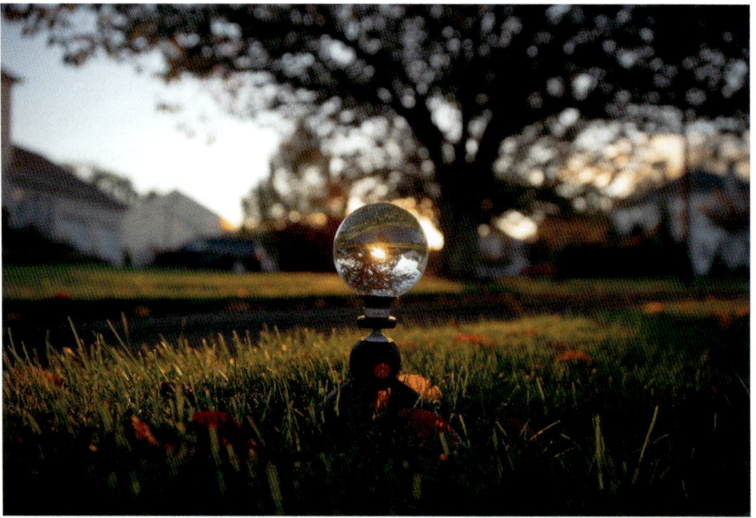

35mm

The 35mm focal length moves us into the wide, portrait category. This lens is wide but not too wide, and is an excellent all-around lens for street photography. Because this is wider than "normal," you will have more opportunities to capture more of the background to tell a better story while still drawing attention to the main subject. Since most digital cameras have higher resolutions at their disposal, you can always crop for a more detailed frame without sacrificing much image quality.

The field of view at this focal length manages to avoid a good amount of distortion and still produce images with a shallow depth of field. Also, the focusing distance works great for handheld lensball shots if you do end up using a prime version of this lens. The further up you move in telephoto lenses, the longer the minimum focus distance they will require.

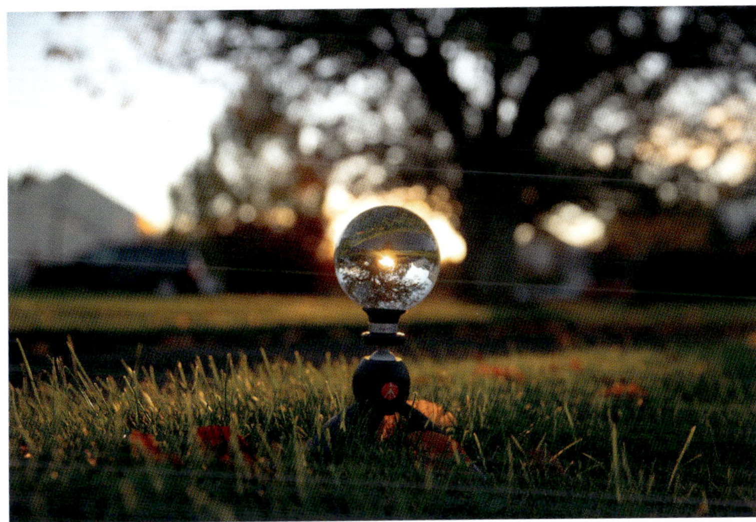

Figure 3.4
35mm | f/2.8 | 1/250s | ISO 100

50mm

The 50mm focal length on a full-frame camera has a very similar field of vision to what your eyes provide. Many photographers refer to this as a medium/natural lens, not wide nor telephoto. Subjects in front of the camera will not look closer or farther away than they actually are. In my experience, the 50mm prime is the best lens to learn composition and framing with. From here, you can experiment with whether you want your images to look more compressed or spread out, allowing you to make informed decisions on your next focal length.

In terms of lensball photography, the 50mm focal length offers an excellent balance of the background and the details within the ball. If you compare figure 3.5 with figure 3.4, you will notice the details in the back become flat rather than stretched and warped. As you use longer telephoto lenses, the backdrop will appear flatter and more compressed.

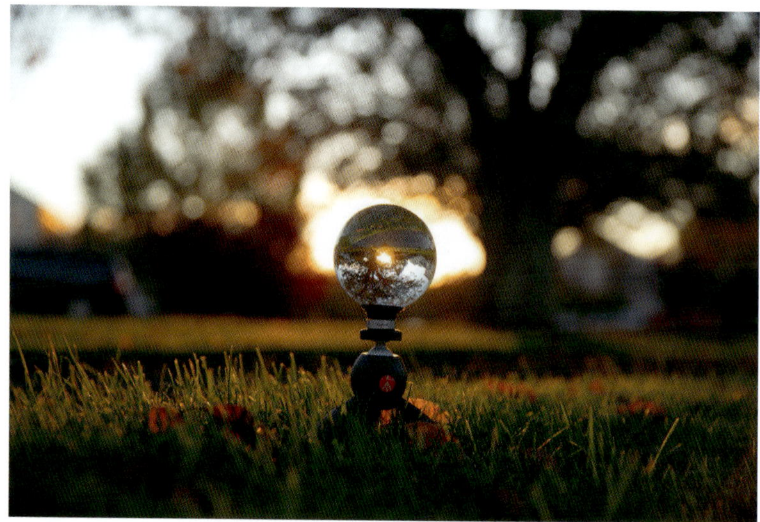

70mm

The 70–85mm focal range is where most portrait photographers comfortably reside. This is the starting point to the realm of telephoto lenses and is great for subject separation. However, in order to keep the lensball within the frame of the shot, you will need to position yourself farther away from the subject to achieve a composition similar to what you would get with a wider-angle lens.

I capture a lot of my lensball photos at 70mm because I love incorporating the falloff at the edge of the ball into the compressed background of the image. Shooting handheld also gets fairly difficult with this focal length, as the minimum focusing distance is almost the length of my arm. As mentioned earlier, a drawback of shooting with telephoto lenses is the apparent introduction of camera shake or motion blur in your pictures. Be sure to compensate by either shooting with high-speed multi-shot settings or bumping up the ISO for a faster shutter speed.

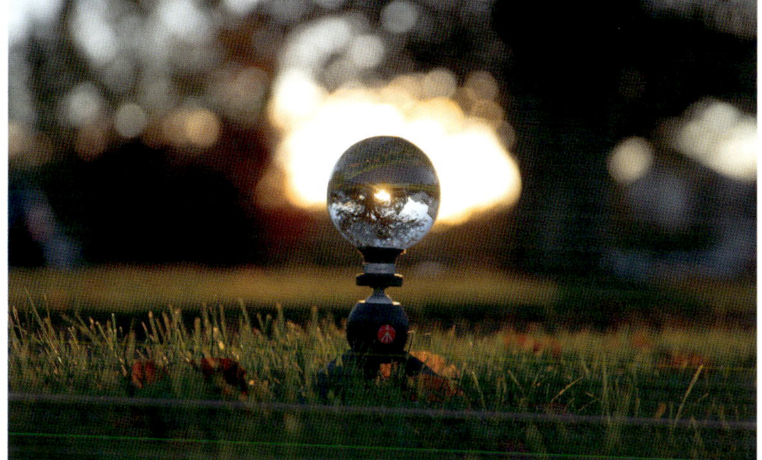

100mm

Shooting at 100mm will require you to be a few feet away from the ball in order to capture the entire subject in the frame. The purpose of shooting past 70mm is to bring out more detail within the ball, at the expense of blurring out the background. I would reserve this telephoto for shooting something really interesting like a pattern or a subject inside the lensball, and using the background blur to avoid any distractions or unwanted elements. A 100mm lens is commonly known as a go-to macro lens, which basically means it gives you an insanely close focusing distance. The purpose of shooting a lensball this close would be to capture just the refracted image. You may not even see the edges, depending on how close up you compose for.

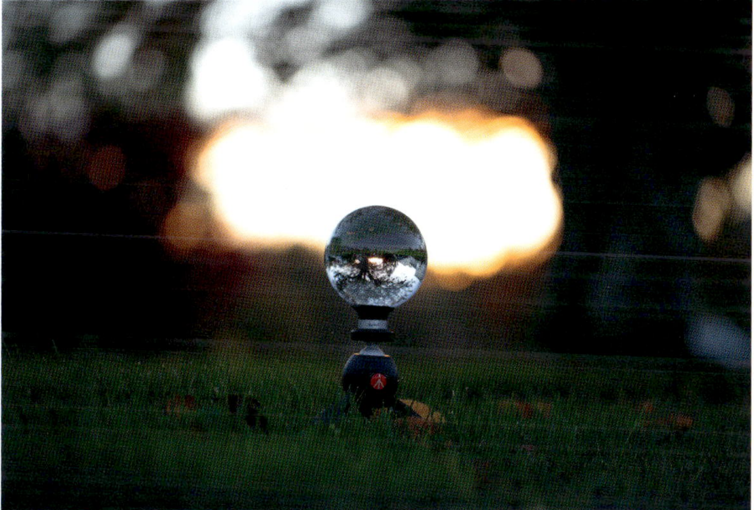

200mm

Now we're moving on to the limits of what I would even consider using during a lensball photoshoot. The 200mm focal length is commonly known as the maximum focal length of most classic telephoto lenses. I had to move back at least five feet in order to capture the ball within the similar frame set. As you can see, the background has been blurred out to oblivion and the bokeh is actually the small opening in the tree. I typically have to raise my ISO to around 200–400 when shooting at this focal length. Photographing at 200mm can help you achieve a dreamy look, but will make it more difficult to plan out the composition, depending on what's behind the lensball.

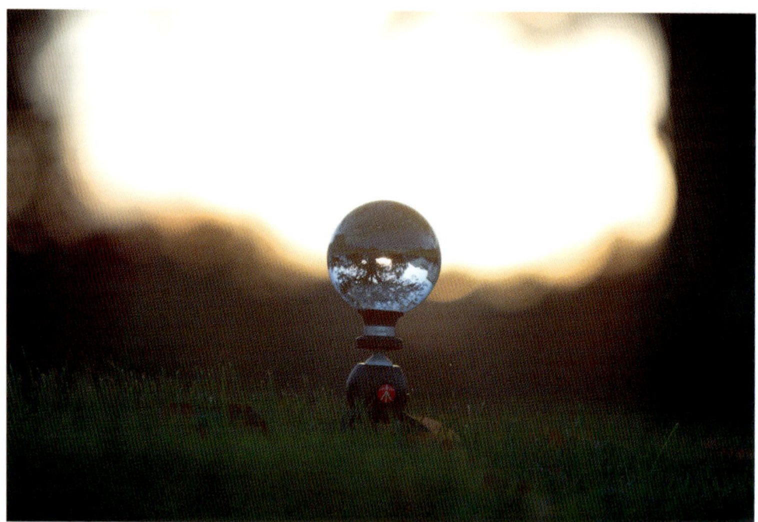

400mm

I don't know why you would use a 400mm lens to shoot a lensball, but I might as well include it in the list. The lens I shot this with is generally used for photographing birds or planes. Due to the properties of this 100–400mm lens, the lowest aperture is f/4.5–f/5.6, based on the zoom length, respectively. To capture a similar composition, you will need to be positioned around 10 to 12 feet away from the subject. Although you do get very nice bokeh, you lose almost all detail in the background and will basically be taking a warped, upside-down image of the scenery through a glass ball.

So Which Lens Should You Choose?

One thing you will notice when shooting with various focal lengths is that the composition inside the sphere does not change as drastically as the compression behind the ball. This is primarily because the inside image is affected by the distance between the ball and the environment, whereas the compression of the background relates to the distance between the camera and the lensball.

Typically, I would choose a wide focal length when the overall scene is the main focus of the capture and the refraction within the ball is not too interesting. This is where external leading lines and landscapes are utilized to help tell a story or guide the audience toward the subject. Telephoto lenses should be reserved for a more isolated look where you want to eliminate all background distractions. For this, I use a focal length between 50mm and 70mm when the background does not work too well with the composition, but I want to capture the inside of the ball as much as I can.

The lens I keep on my camera when shooting with lensball is the Canon 24–70mm f/2.8 L series lens. I never have a need to go wider or narrower than the range this offers, and the focusing distance is perfect for handheld shots. I also enjoy the versatility of being able to cycle through different focal lengths without having to dig through my bag and swap lenses on location. You may hear some pushback from prime lens shooters, as they would argue a fixed focal length will coerce you to be more creative, which I do agree with, but this may come with the sacrifice of missing a once-in-a-moment photo. Additionally, the minimum focusing distance of some prime lenses can make it very difficult to capture lensball images up close. I would definitely recommend confirming these limitations before dropping money on a new lens.

My Lensball Travel Kit

I primarily shoot with a Sony a7R II mirrorless camera with a Canon 24–70mm f/2.8 L series lens and a Metabones adapter. I try my best to travel light and most of my equipment can fit inside a messenger bag or sling.

When I first began shooting with a lensball, I would just drop it in with the rest of my camera equipment when I was heading out for a shoot. I didn't really conduct any planning and would just snap a shot when I found it convenient. Throughout the years, I've tried out

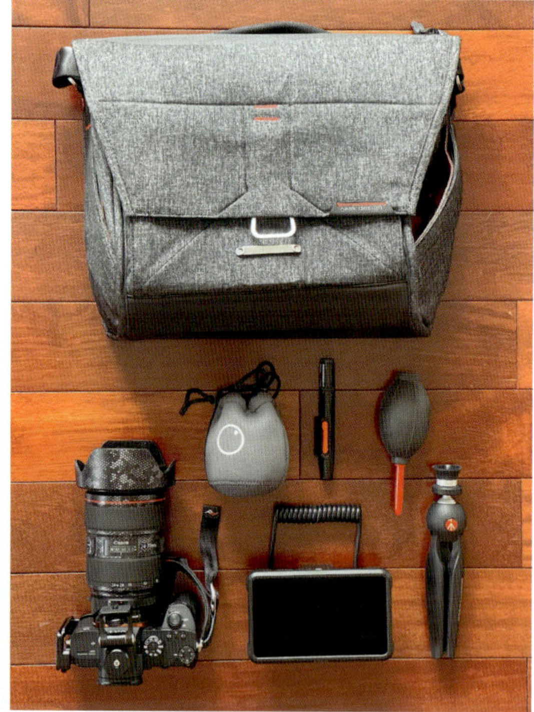

Figure 3.10

My kit consists of a Canon 24–70mm lens, Sony a7R II mirrorless camera body, Lensball, external monitor, mini tripod with a Lensball mount, and a cleaning kit. All of these items fit perfectly in my Peak Design messenger bag for a lightweight day carry.

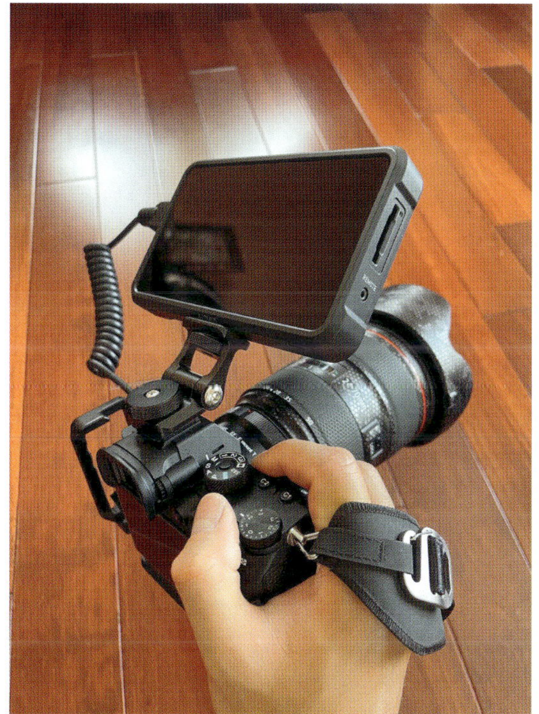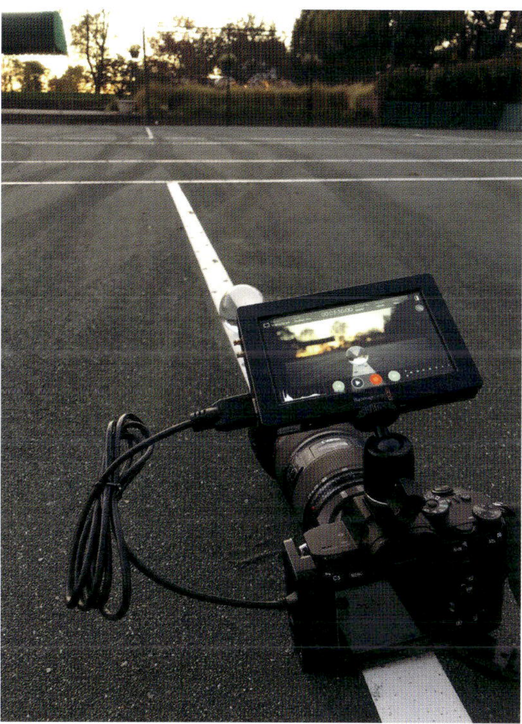

Figure 3.11a

Figure 3.11b

I mount an Atomos Shinobi external monitor on my camera, which gives me a much better view of the framing for each shot.

different tools to see what works well with my workflow and what items are necessary to bring on location. As shown in figure 3.10, I currently have a dedicated messenger bag for when I have certain concepts or places I want to shoot in mind. I prefer not to lug around a large backpack unless I am planning on bringing multiple lenses.

For most of my shoots, I attach an external monitor to the camera so I can get a clearer view of my composition and focus (figures 3.11a and 3.11b). A lot of my lensball photos require me to place the ball on the ground and there were times when the flip-out screen wasn't doing it for me. Using an external monitor does improve my workflow, as I can see the framing much clearer. The one I currently use is the Atomos Shinobi and it is super helpful when capturing video or taking self-portraits. The screen is significantly brighter than the LCD on the back of my camera, allowing me to accurately set the exposure on a sunny day. Some monitors also have helpful tools like large histograms and zebra-stripe exposure warnings. Having this additional monitor does add a good amount of weight to the camera and will be an excellent workout for your forearm.

For instances where there is uneven terrain or unstable ground, I have the lensball sit on a silicon mount from Lensball (figure 3.13). This is attached to a small Manfrotto tripod with a ball-mount head. This setup is ideal to use if you need to capture a photo where the lensball is eye level to the camera.

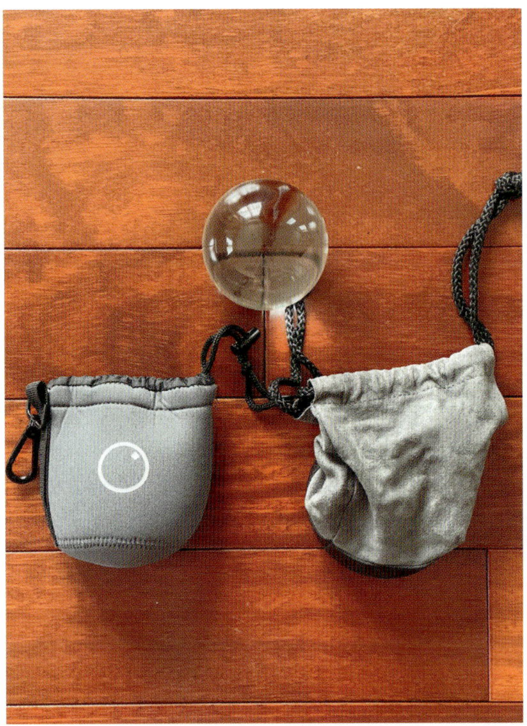

Figure 3.12
I suggest upgrading the bag for your lensball, as the one it comes with isn't the best. I've had some luck with a Camera Lens bag (right) for a while. It protected the ball from scratches and, surprisingly, even from drops. However, the newer one from Lensball (left) is even better and is currently is my go-to carrier. It has a cinch cord and carabiner so you can latch it onto your camera bag or strap.

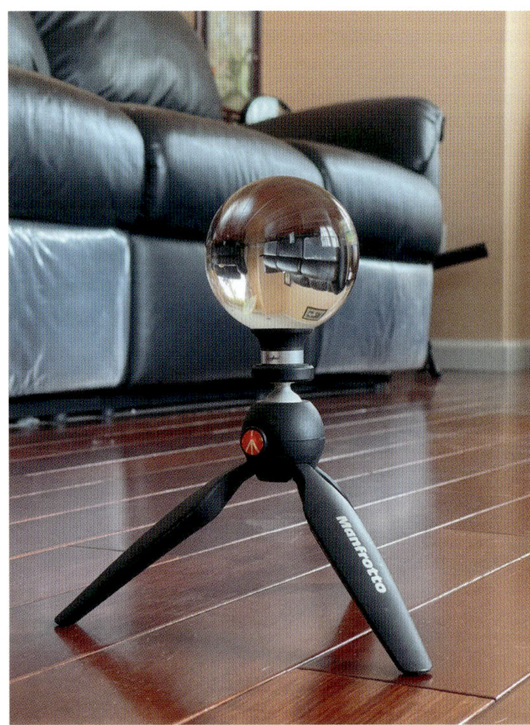

Figure 3.13
My lensball atop a silicon mount attached to a tripod. There is nothing too special about this setup, other than that it is portable and sleek.

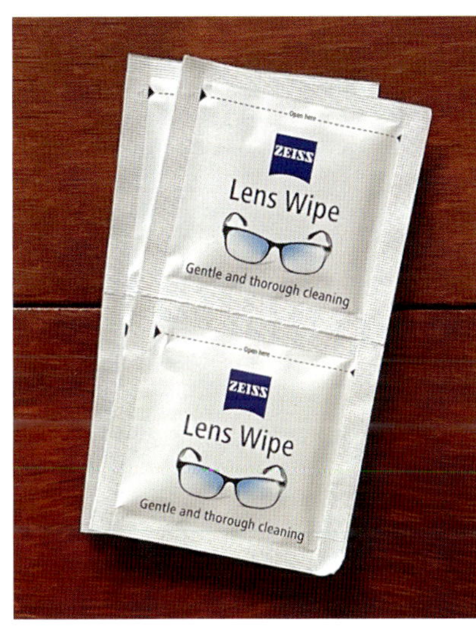

Figure 3.14
I always carry some cleaning supplies to ensure the lensball and camera are spotless. I found that the Lens Wipes from Zeiss work really well on the glass and are fairly cheap for a large box. You can find these in the camera aisle at Walmart. I also bring a dust blower and a lens pen to remove any debris from the ball without repositioning it and ruining the composition.

All of these items fit perfectly into a 13-inch messenger bag and make it easy to access in most scenarios on location. Try out different tools and setups to see what works best for your workflow.

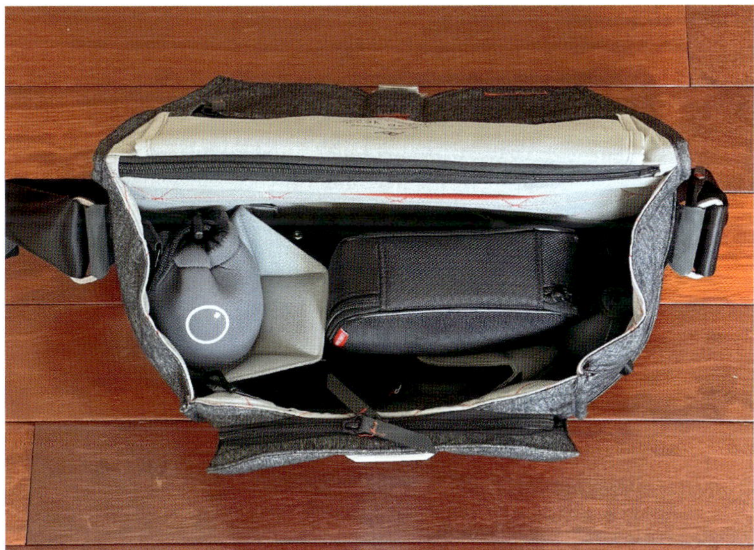

Figure 3.15

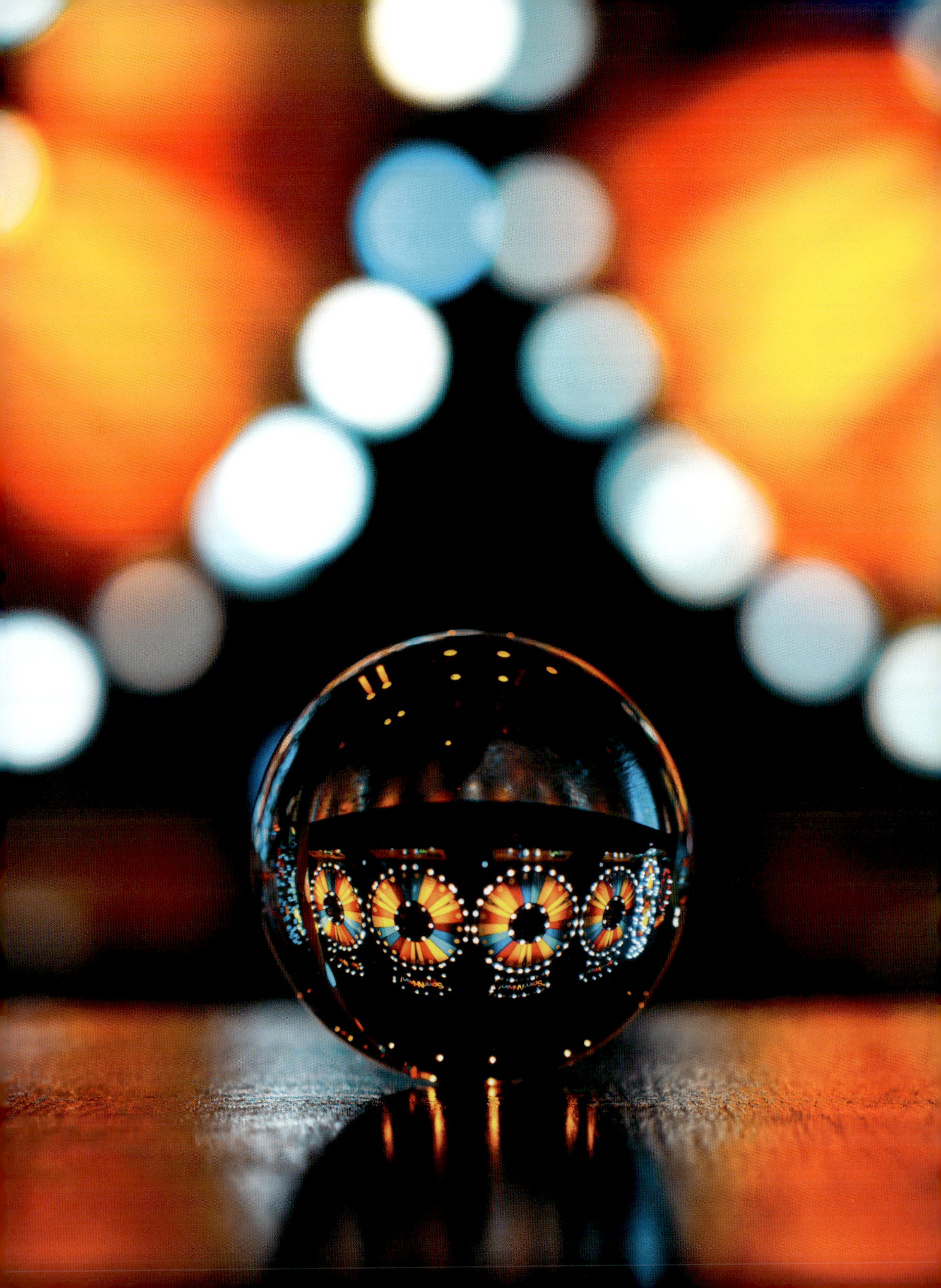

CHAPTER 4

Contrast with Color

Typically, photographers understand contrast as the difference between light and dark. Specifically, it is the gap between the lightest lights and the darkest darks. In post-processing, modifying contrast can make a photo look more vivid and intense, or more muted and soft. Color contrast, however, is described as using different dominant colors to create separation, or contrast, in an image. There are many variations of how certain colors can make or break an image. If used correctly, specific combinations can add definition to your photo and make it stand out (figures 4.1a and 4.1b).

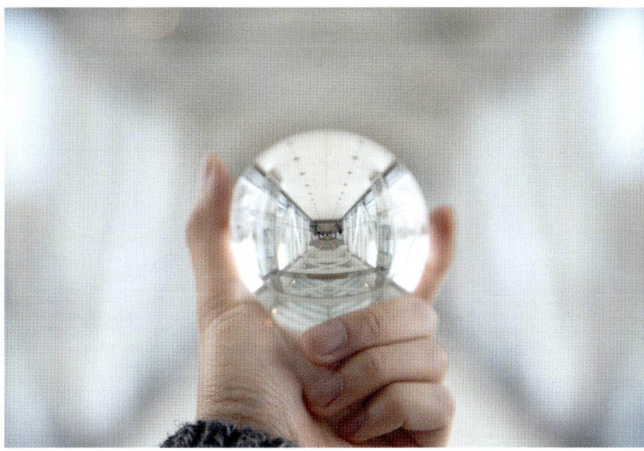

Figure 4.1a

70mm | F/2.8 | 1/125s | ISO 100

A lack of color contrast can make an image feel dull and lifeless, as seen in figure 4.1a. Figure 4.1b exemplifies strong blue and orange tones, which we will later describe as complementary colors. This helps attract the viewer's eyes to the photo. The lack of a dominant color scheme in the first shot can be hard to work with in post-processing.

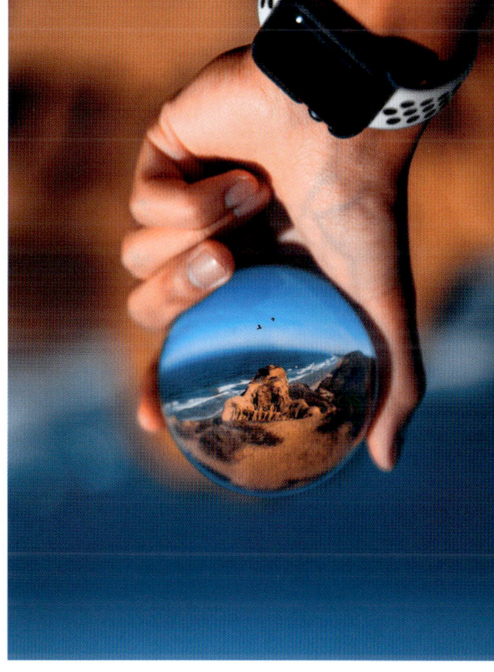

Figure 4.1b

70mm | F/2.8 | 1/5000s | ISO 100

You may not think much of it, but color plays a huge role in how we perceive an image. If used purposefully, each color can allude to specific emotions or moods. For example, films are generally shot with two dominant colors, as this gives the cinematographer more control over setting the tone of the scene. This is no different in photography, and if used correctly, this effect can strengthen your image. In this chapter, I'll cover some different color guides I use often when planning a shot as well as during post-processing.

One of the key elements to creating the perfect image is utilizing the appropriate camera settings for your vision. I won't go too deep into explaining how to balance the exposure triangle, but there are some basic settings all photographers need to keep in mind during a shoot: aperture, shutter speed, and ISO. I capture most of my images in manual mode and configure the settings in the order mentioned. While it is not necessary to shoot in manual mode to photograph a lensball, it will save you some headache to nail the shot.

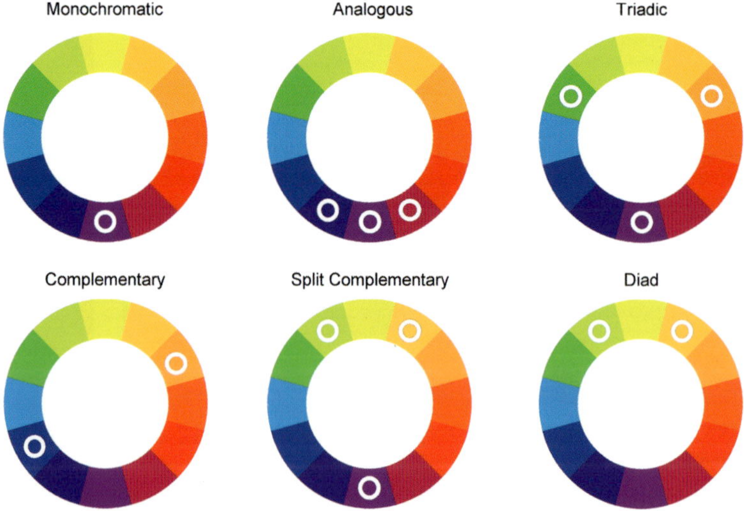

Figure 4.2

Most of you have seen some form of the color wheel, which illustrates the separate color hues in a circle. There are a number of unique color combinations artists use to help tell a story or convey an emotion. In most of my lensball work, I focus on monochromatic, diadic, and complementary colors to set a theme for the overall image.

Monochromatic

This color scheme, as the name suggests, uses only one dominant color to dictate the feel of the image. You can argue that this is the opposite of color contrast, as there aren't any other colors to contrast with; however, you are free to utilize colors within the similar palette.

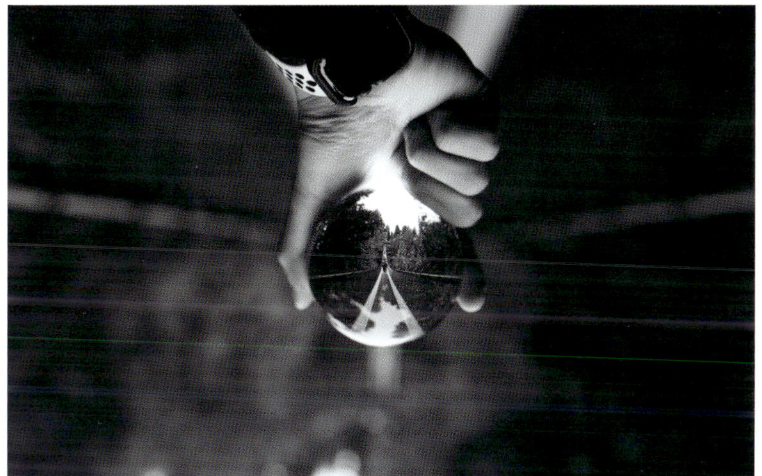

Figure 4.3a

35mm | F/2.8 | 1/200s | ISO 100

Black-and-white photographs devoid of color draw focus to lighting, composition, and texture. You effectively present the feel and the shape of the scene without the common distraction of color. What makes these photographs stand out is that they take away something you see every day and force you into a medium where you pay closer attention to different details.

Figure 4.3b

35mm | F/2.8 | 1/100s | ISO 125

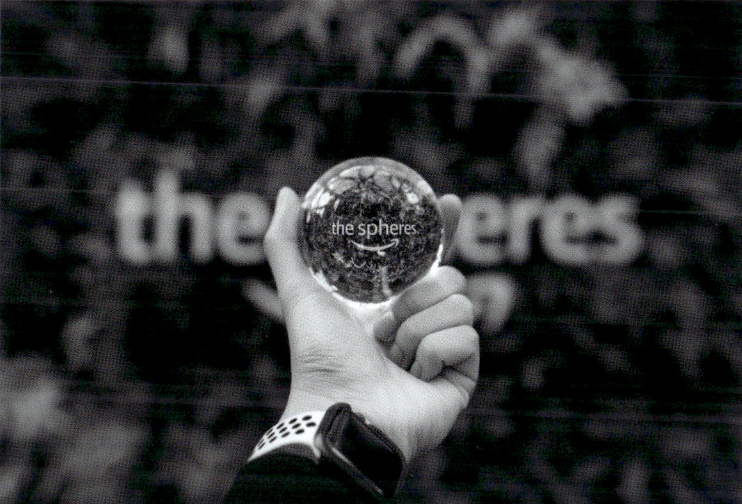

You can also have other colors present in the photo as long as they don't compete with the primary color.

The reason you would go this route is to produce a smooth, easy on the eyes photograph. Unlike a black-and-white image (figures 4.3a and 4.3b), where subjects and lighting are emphasized without the distraction of color, a monochromatic color scheme adds an additional layer of storytelling (figures 4.4a and 4.4b).

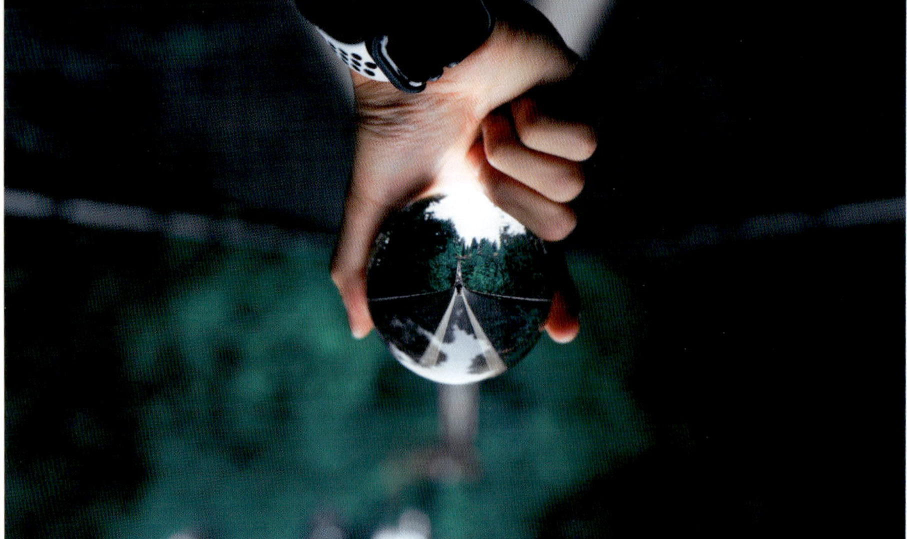

Figure 4.4a

35mm | F/2.8 | 1/200s | ISO 100

Monochromatic photos present the image similarly to black-and-white, but there is more context in either the foreground or background. Things like snow and sand can look very similar in photos, but when their color is given a push to either blue or yellow, the viewer gets a clearer idea of what they're looking at. When comparing the figures 4.4a and 4.4b to their respective black-and-white counterparts (figures 4.3a and 4.3b), you will notice the blue-green hue gives you the notion that the photo was captured in a forest or in front of foliage.

Figure 4.4b

35mm | F/2.8 | 1/100s | ISO 125

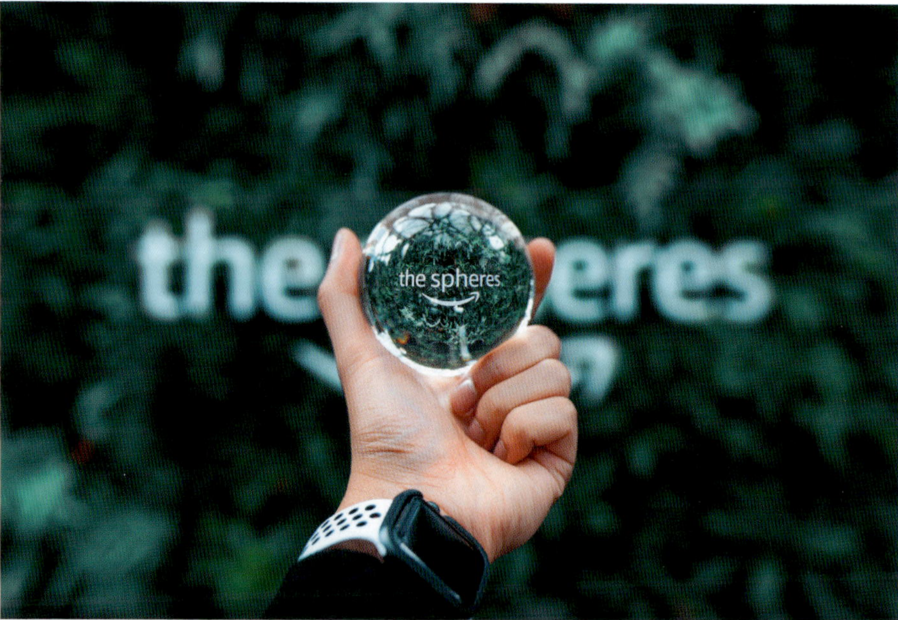

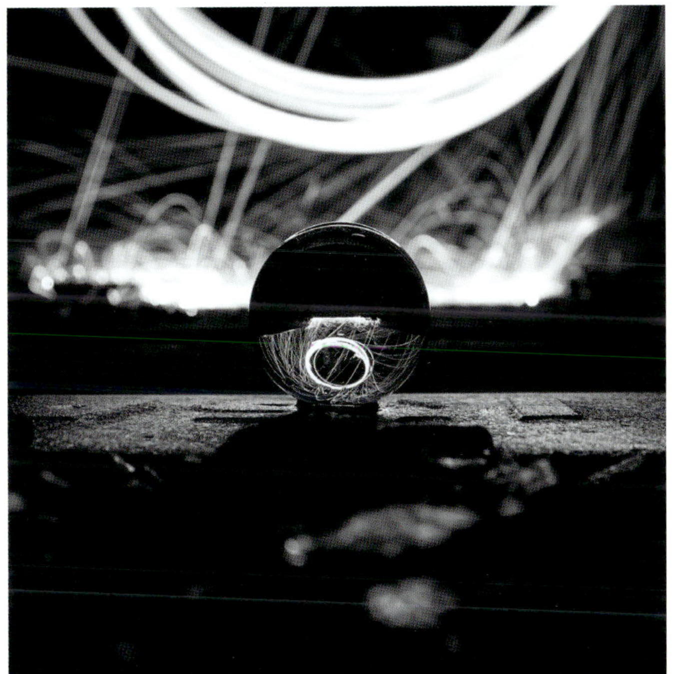

Figure 4.5a

24mm | F/4.0 | 4.6s | ISO 100

This is another great example of a monochromatic edit. Figure 4.5a shows a strong definition of the image where it is structured by only whites, grays, and blacks. The source of light may be ambiguous, and it is up to the audience to guess if it is a cool or warm photo. Introducing a blue hue in figure 4.5b alters the feel of the photo, creating a cold ambience.

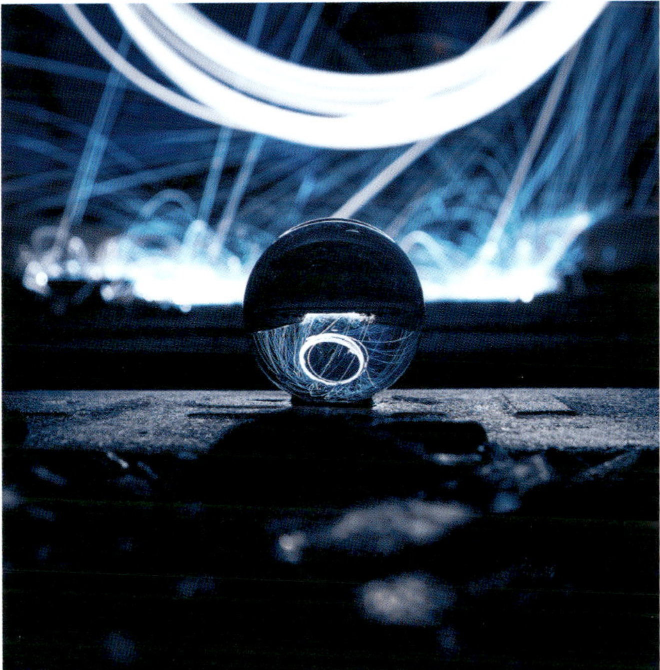

Figure 4.5b

24mm | F/4.0 | 4.6s | ISO 100

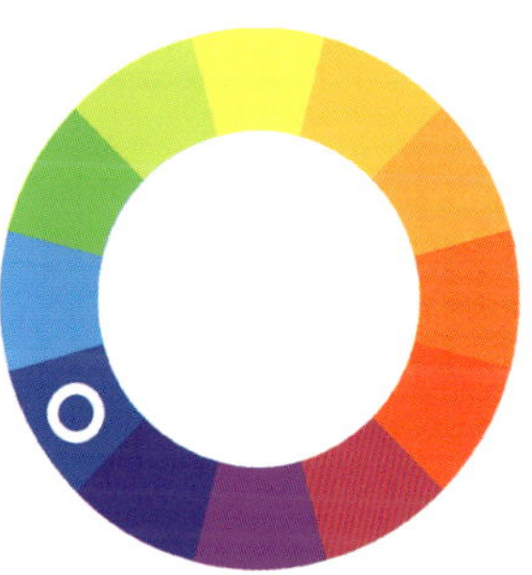

Figure 4.5c

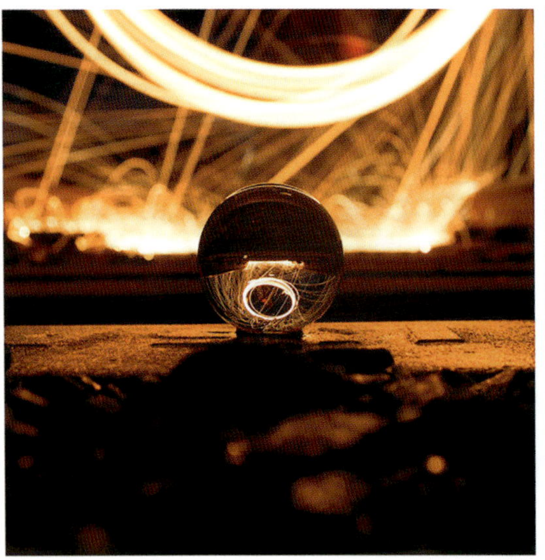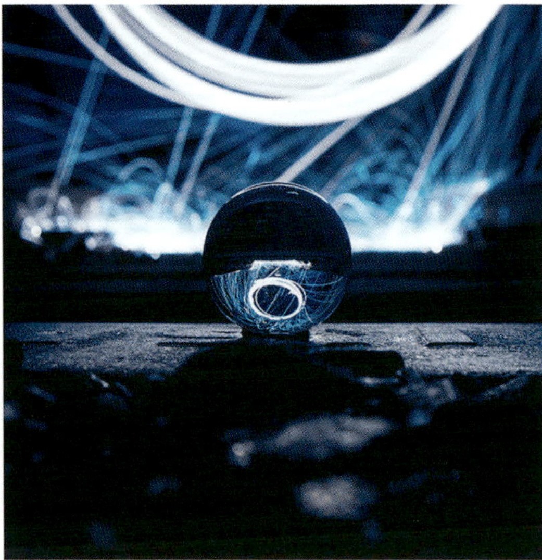

Figure 4.5d

24mm | F/4.0 | 4.6s | ISO 100

I created the light in the background of this photo by swinging lit steel wool tied to a whisk with a long chain. Slowing down the shutter speed to around 4.6 seconds allowed the sensor to be exposed to the light longer, producing the halo effect. The camera was manually focused on the lensball where I would have been standing. If you are shooting in the dark, it is advisable to use a flashlight or lit object to mark your position while focusing behind the camera. Steel wool naturally burns with a yellow-orange hue, but I cooled down the image in post-processing to make it stand out. Also, I must give you a fair warning not to light steel wool in dry areas or public places, as it can start fires if you're not careful.

Figure 4.6a

70mm | F/2.8 | 1/320s | ISO 100

This monochromatic capture of the Manhattan Bridge empha-sizes the brown and orange colors in the bricks and skin. Although the black-and-white photo brings out the sharp details in the image, the colored photo (figure 4.6b) provides the viewer data into the cold, cloudy weather conditions in which the image was shot, along with the rustic urban aes-thetic of the street. Both images can stand well on their own, but each can be used to exemplify a different feeling.

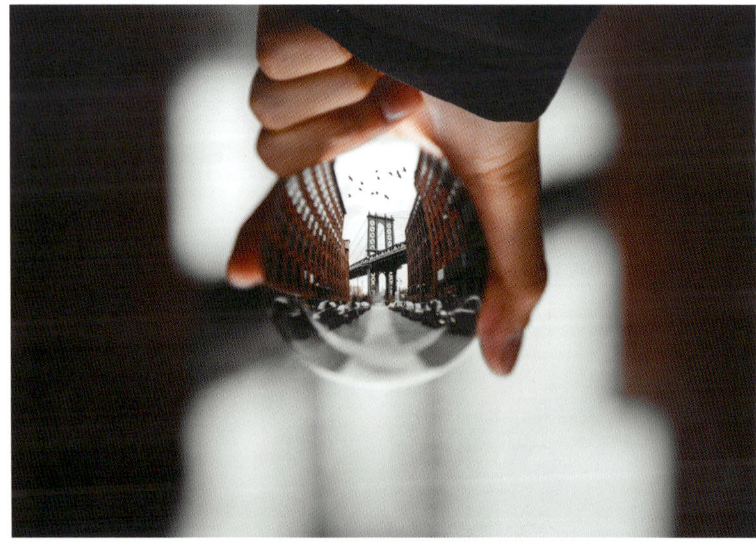

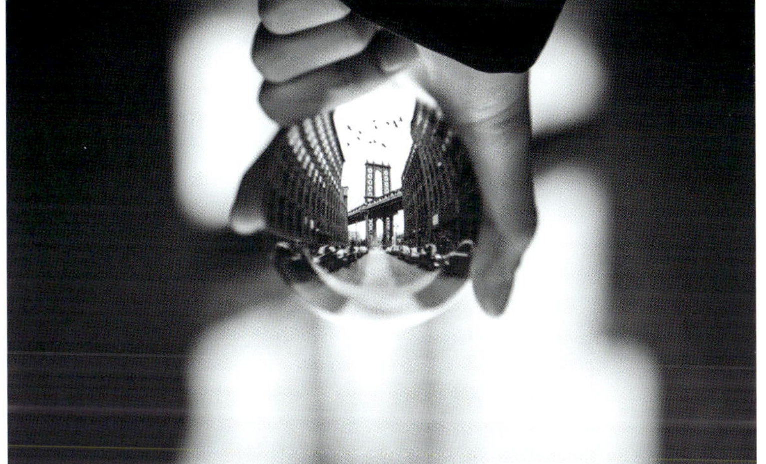

Diad

The diad color scheme is described as using two colors that are separated by an adjacent color. For example, blue and violet are divided by blue-violet in the color wheel (figure 4.7). Similar to monochromatic photos, diadic colors still reside on the same end of the color wheel but add a subtle layer of color separation with the additional hue. I typically use this combination when color grading "blue hour" photos where color contrast is lost just as or right after the sun sets (figure 4.8). It may be difficult to find harmonic diadic colors in nature, so another option can be to emphasize them in post-processing. There are many unique photo-editing tools you can use to stretch similar colors into distinct hues (figures 4.9a and 4.9b). I will discuss this later in the photo-editing portion of the book (pages 78–84).

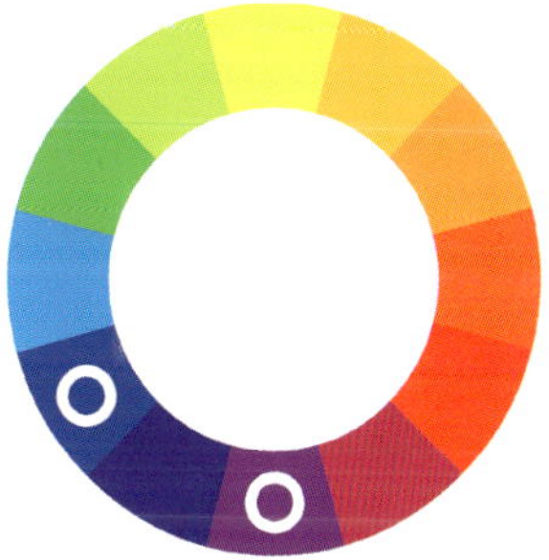

Figure 4.7
Blue and violet are diadic colors—they are separated by one color on the color wheel. Other examples include blue and green, red and orange, etc.

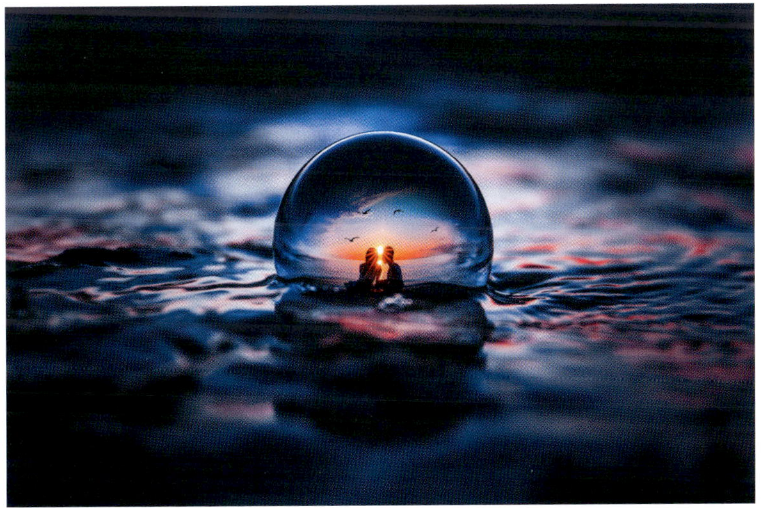

Figure 4.8
70mm | F/2.8 | 1/125s | ISO 100
The colors captured during "blue hour" are relatively similar, ranging from light blue to almost magenta. This photo is a composite—the inner ball image was captured during sunset and color-matched to the background image, which was captured as the sun dipped below the horizon.

Colors can be stretched into separate hues depending on how they were captured in the original photo. Typically, steel-wool long exposures include colors within the yellow to orange spectrum. For this image, the temperature was cooled to 2250 kelvin and the magenta tint was brought up, revealing a color diad of blue and magenta rather than the monochromatic version with only light orange.

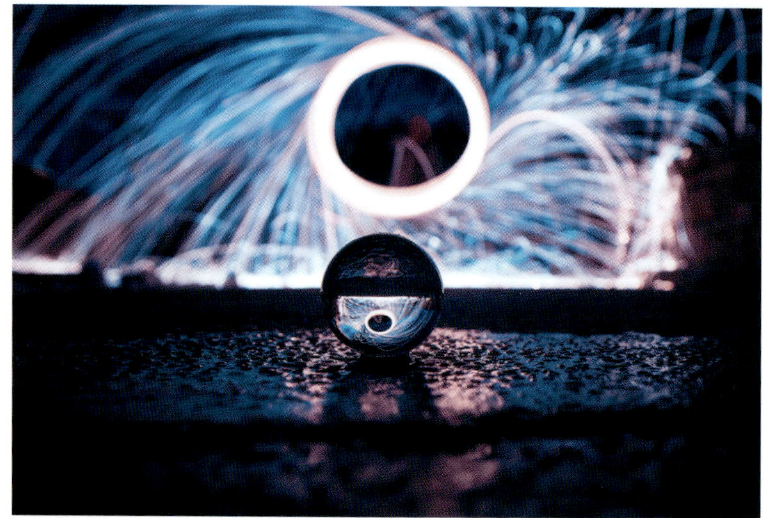

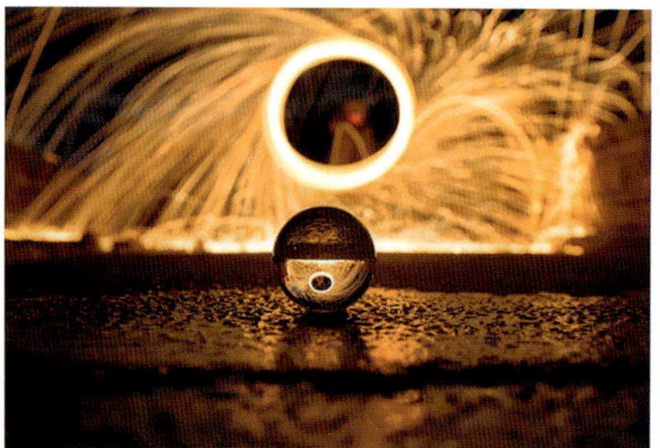
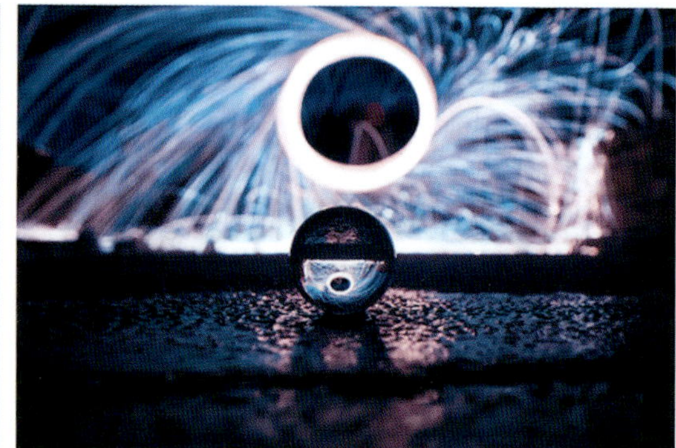

Figure 4.9b

Complementary

Complementary colors refer to two colors on the opposite ends of the color wheel. This color configuration makes your photos appear brighter and more prominent because of the high-contrast look it creates. You may notice this color scheme in everyday pop culture art, as it is very eye-catching and can be found commonly in nature. When I shoot lensball photos, I usually look for existing cool and warm hues in the environment. This is the easiest way to create strong color contrast when post-processing, as the colors will not bleed into each other when adjusting hues. Some examples can be found in the yellow-orange warmth of a sunset in conjunction with the crisp light blue of the sky, or the flowery pink tones of a cherry blossom accompanied by the vivid green in the leaves. There are many combinations of colors you can play with, and once you have a solid understanding of them, you will be able to recreate this look in any photo.

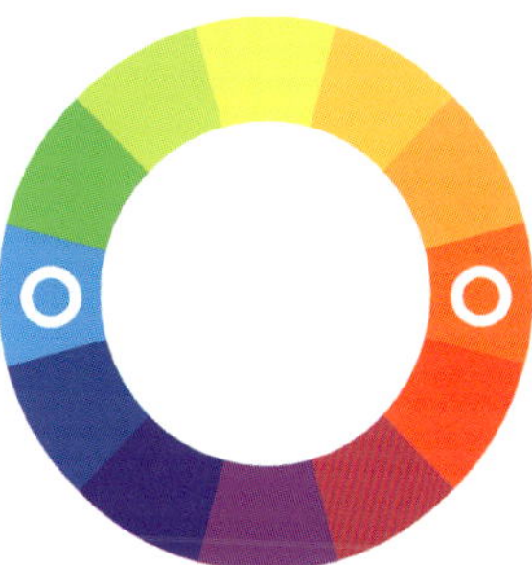

Figure 4.10
Complementary colors represent any two colors that are directly opposite each other on the color wheel. Orange and teal are very common complementary colors used in photography.

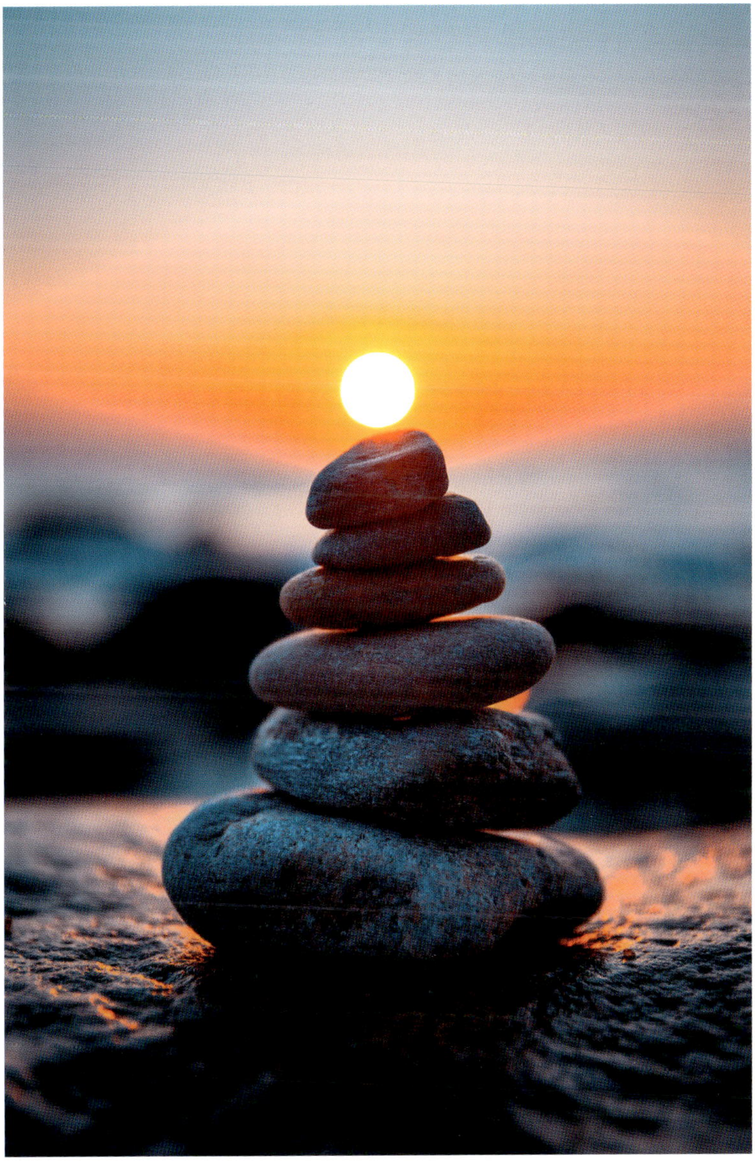

Figure 4.11
42mm | F/2.8 | 1/800s | ISO 100
Orange and teal are prevalent complementary colors found in nature. This sunrise photo uses these colors to create a strong contrast in the photo. Not much post-processing was needed, as the colors were present in the original shot.

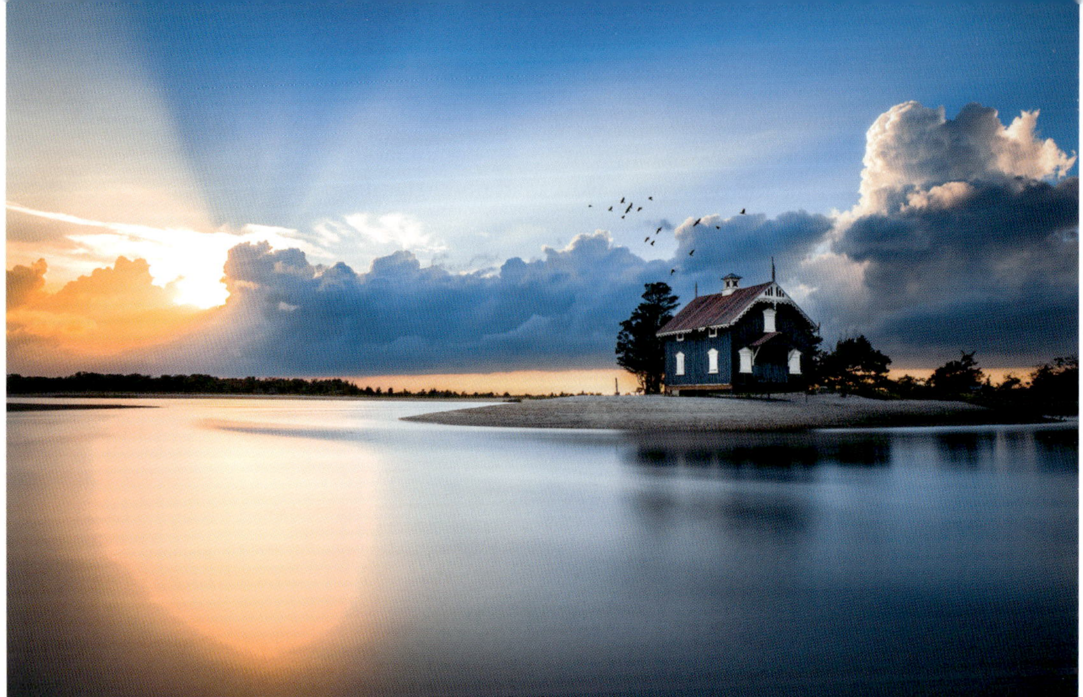

Figure 4.12

Complementary colors can also be used to set a gradient that helps divide the image. This capture of a nearby beach shed during sunset is separated by the warm tones on the left and the cool tones on the right.

Figure 4.13

The divided colors can be attributed to highlights and shadows to add an additional layer of contrast. In this photo, the golden orange tones boost the highlights and the dark blues reside in the shadows.

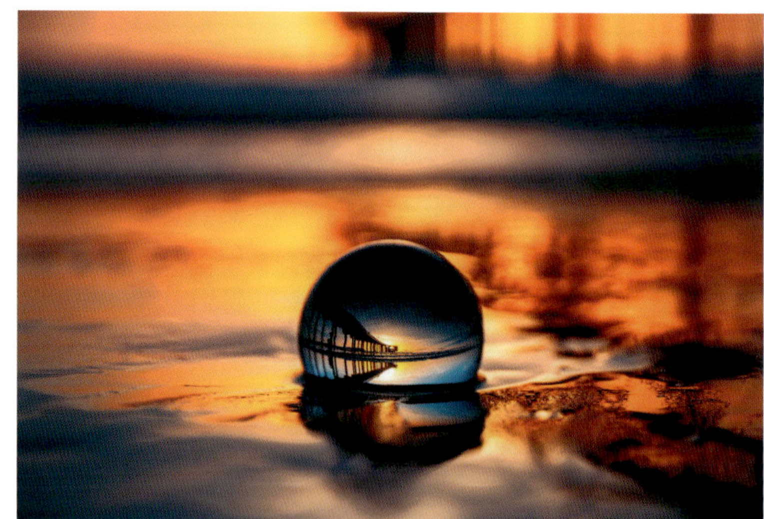

CHAPTER 5

Crafting Composition

Composition is one of the most widely discussed and subjective topics in photography. First off, we need to understand what exactly a photograph is. Whenever you take a photograph, you are essentially capturing a three-dimensional space in a two-dimensional visual. Composition helps you explain how certain subjects fit within the frame and, in better terms, tell a story of why they are there and why they are important.

Although you may have the technical knowledge necessary to properly expose an image, there are a number of different ways to compose it. You may hear other artists mention compositional principles like the rule of thirds, leading lines, or repeating patterns, but these should be treated more as guidelines than rules. It is one thing to use these tactics to make your photos stand out, but to follow them strictly can be limiting and unnecessary. Once you have a good understanding of the basics of composition, you can find ways to move around or improve upon them.

Composing images can be done in camera or during post-processing with the crop tool, but it is best to get as close as you can to your desired framing on location. In this chapter, I'll cover some of the key elements of composition I find helpful and discuss how to incorporate them into your lensball photos.

What Is Composition and Why Is It Important?

In the simplest terms, composition is the selective arrangement of objects to guide your viewer's eyes around an image. These photographic elements are meant to give the scene purpose or be used as a medium for storytelling. Even things like shadows and highlights can be used as lines to divide a picture or lead the viewer's eyes toward a subject. Although the definition is fairly straightforward, it can be difficult to successfully build a strong composition within the environment you are given. There are also many different techniques you can use to achieve this, and I will do my best to break them down as easily as I can.

Rule of Thirds

The rule of thirds is probably the most frequently mentioned compositional technique. This concept involves mentally dividing your image with two horizontal and two vertical lines, creating nine individual squares within the frame (figure 5.1a). You then align the subject or items you want the viewer to notice at one of the intersections of those lines or along the lines themselves. The focus is to build your image with an off-center subject rather than positioning the subject directly in the center. This requires you, as the photographer, to play around with negative space to add interest within the image. The subjects do not have to be perfectly aligned or on the point of intersection, just close enough. For example, in figure 5.1b, the subject is positioned along the rightmost line while attention is also drawn to the birds and cirrus clouds on the top two intersections. The image is also divided by tone, with one-third being warm-toned and two-thirds being cool-toned.

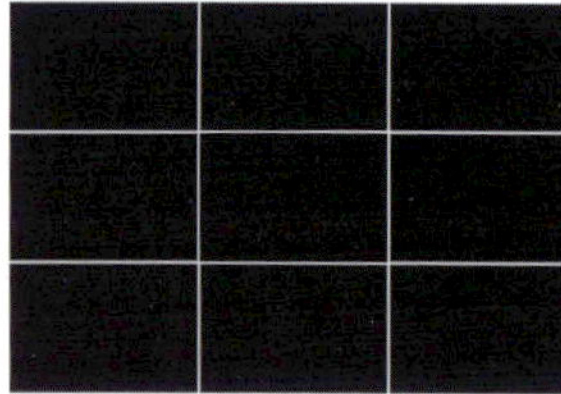

Figure 5.1a
The rule of thirds is one of the most popular guides and the easiest to use for beginners.

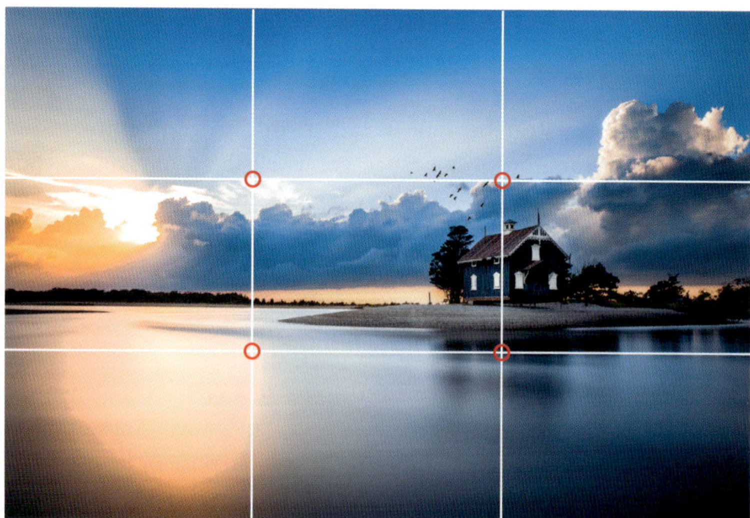

Figure 5.1b
24mm | F/2.8 | 10s | ISO 50
When using the rule of thirds, try your best to frame the shot to include items of visual interest near the lines or intersections to emphasize their impact. You do not need to have something sitting on all four points.

I typically do not use the rule of thirds for positioning the lensball in the frame. Because the image within the ball is largely affected by how offset it is from the center, I try my best to align it directly in the middle of the frame or align it with the top or bottom horizontal lines (figure 5.2a). However, this rule does come in handy when composing everything else in the scene, like the highlights, shadows, and horizon (figure 5.2b).

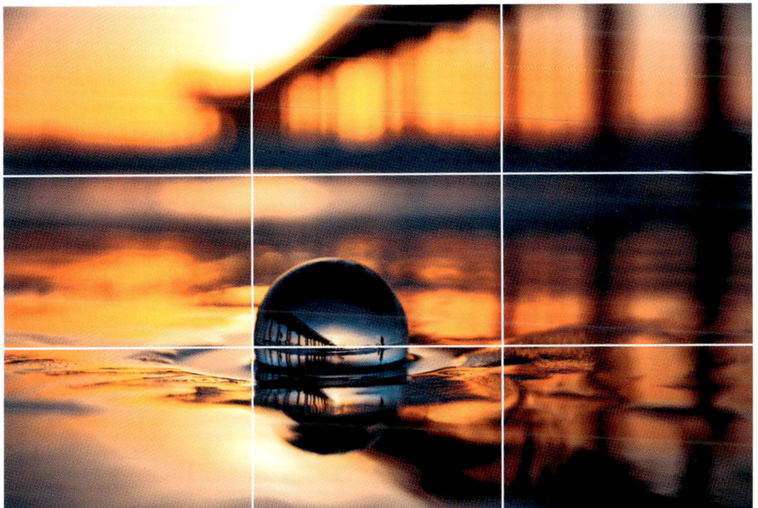

Figure 5.2a

70mm | F/2.8 | 1/2500s | ISO 100
The subject does not have to be perfectly placed on a line or intersection. The rule of thirds can be used to split highlights and shadows or positive space and negative space. Landscape horizons work well when placed along the top or bottom horizontal gridline.

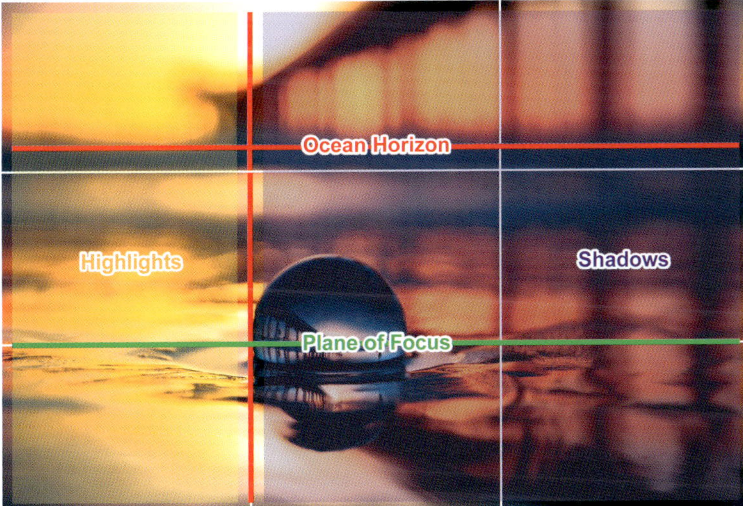

Figure 5.2b

Diagonal Framing

The diagonal method is used to draw the viewer's attention toward the front and center of an image. Similar to the rule of thirds, you want to set up the focus along one of the four bisections; however, with this method the lines of the photo are rotated forty-five degrees and are drawn from each corner. This is one of my favorite compositional techniques for lensball photography because it focuses more within the center vertical line of an image, rather than having the subject offset, as seen in the rule of thirds. Another thing to add is that the rule of thirds works well with older, squarelike aspect ratios, such as the 4×5 or 8×10 framing styles, but it can be limiting when overlaid on top of the more modern 2×3 aspect ratios.

Diagonal framing is great for images that contain, as you'd imagine, diagonal qualities. In figures 5.3b and 5.3c, the lensball is aligned

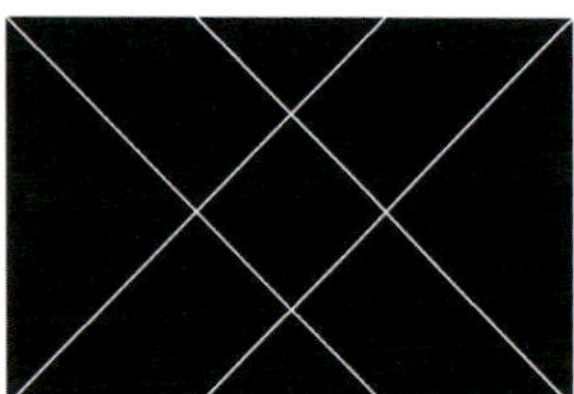

Figure 5.3a

The diagonal lines guide is useful for producing dynamic compositions.

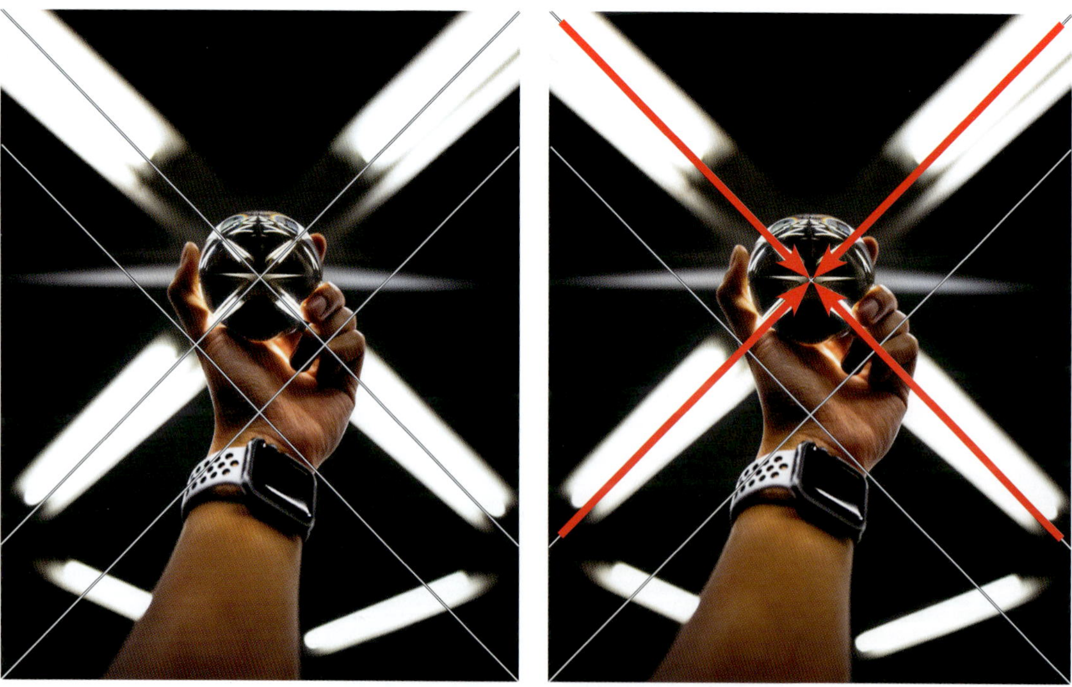

Figure 5.3b

24mm | F/2.8 | 1/320s | ISO 400

This image was captured in a New York City subway station where the ceiling lights criss-crossed. The lines within the ball and behind the ball align well with the diagonal compositional method.

Figure 5.3c

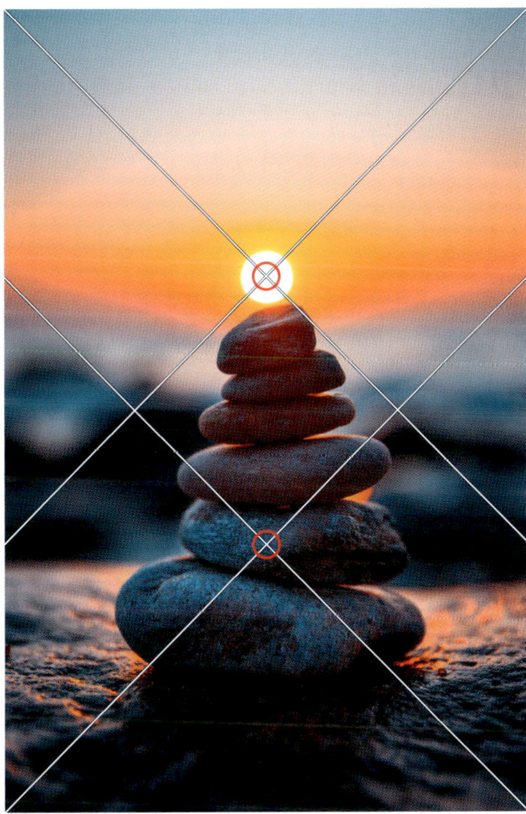

Figure 5.4

42mm | F/2.8 | 1/800s | ISO 100

The diagonal method can be used to guide the eyes to foreground and background elements, like the detail of the rock and the center of the sun.

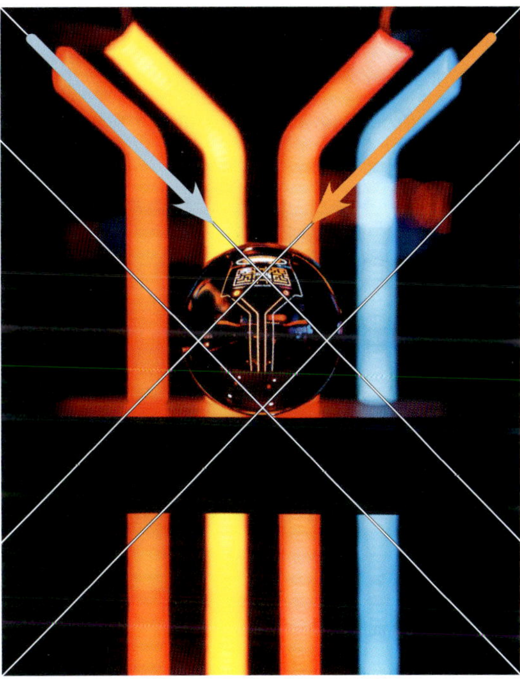

Figure 5.5

85mm | F/2.8 | 1/250s | ISO 800

Another example where the background diagonal lines help emphasize the main subject at the bisection of the top diagonals.

perfectly with the intersection of the ceiling lights, where the center image of the ball is also aligned as well. The double intersection falls on the topmost bisectional point, which helps guide the audience to focus on the detail.

Golden Triangle

The golden triangle approach uses a series of four right triangles to split the image into separate parts. This theory works best with images that contain a strong corner-to-corner diagonal line. For this, you can place points of interest either within each of the separate triangles or along the lines of the triangles. This gives direction to the subject and aligns the viewer's eyes toward the points of interest. You can also use this to implement leading lines in your photos, which we'll discuss later in this chapter.

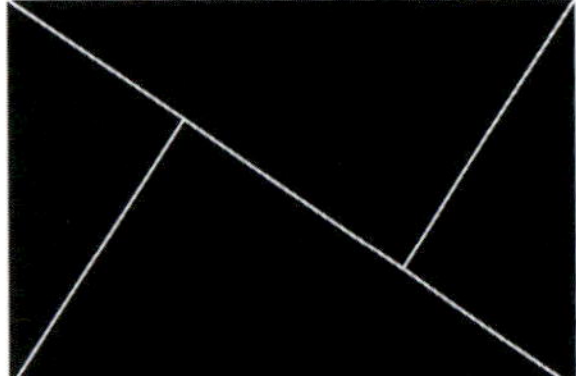

Figure 5.6a
The golden triangle principle utilizes four right triangles to aid image composition.

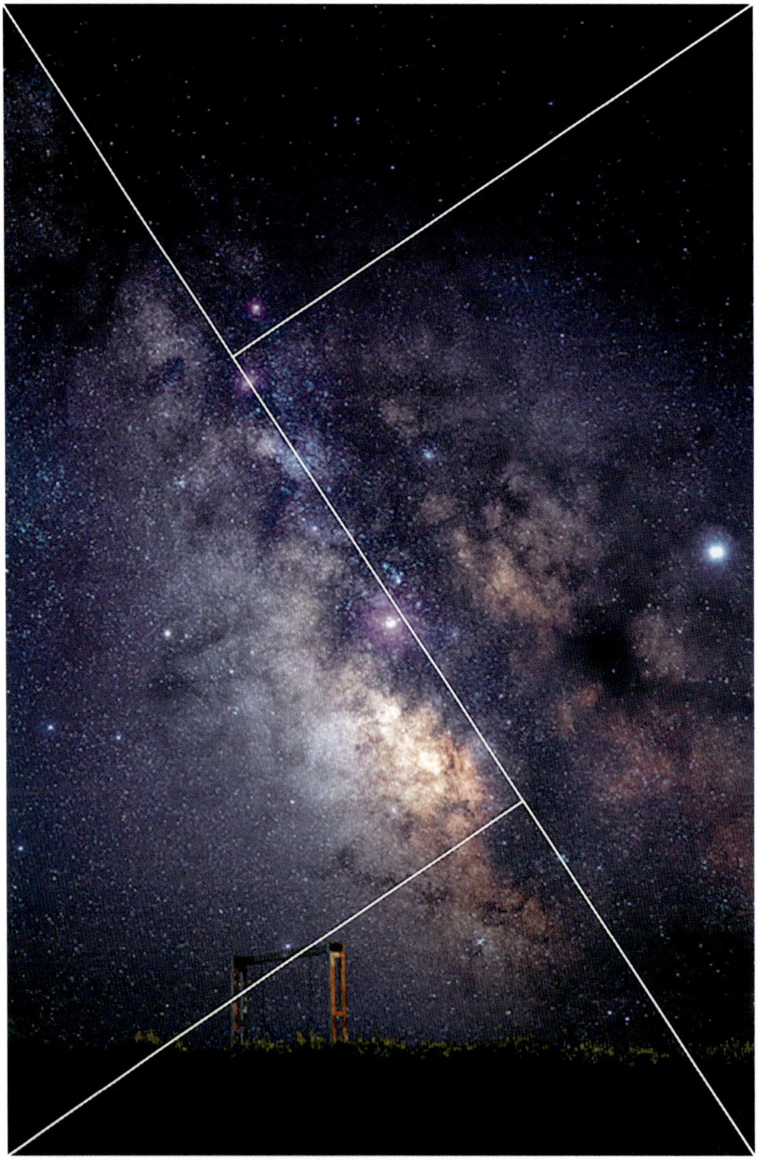

Figure 5.6b
50mm | F/2.5 | 30s | ISO 1600
In this image, the Milky Way is positioned as the dominant diagonal that stretches from the top-left corner down to the bottom-right corner. Objects of interest, such as the swing set, reside on the bottom-left line.

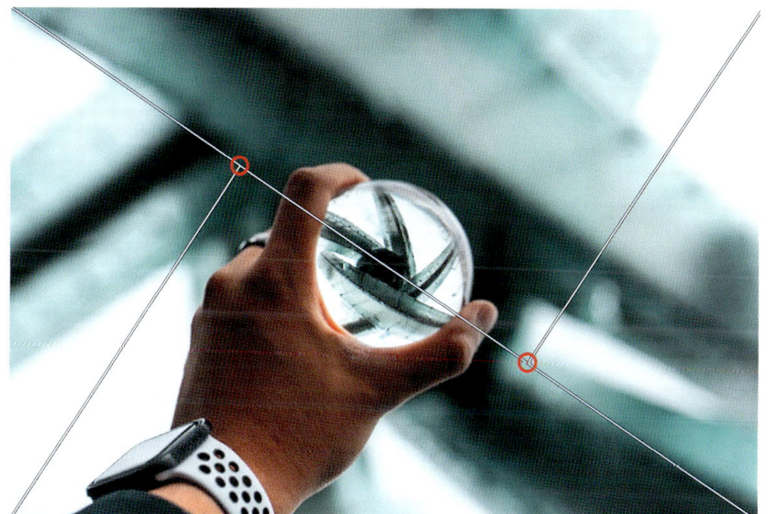

Figure 5.7a

35mm | F/2.8 | 1/1250s | ISO 100

Aligning intersections of the background with the corners of the triangles can help bring balance to a chaotic image.

Figure 5.7b

24mm | F/2.8 | 1/250s | ISO 250

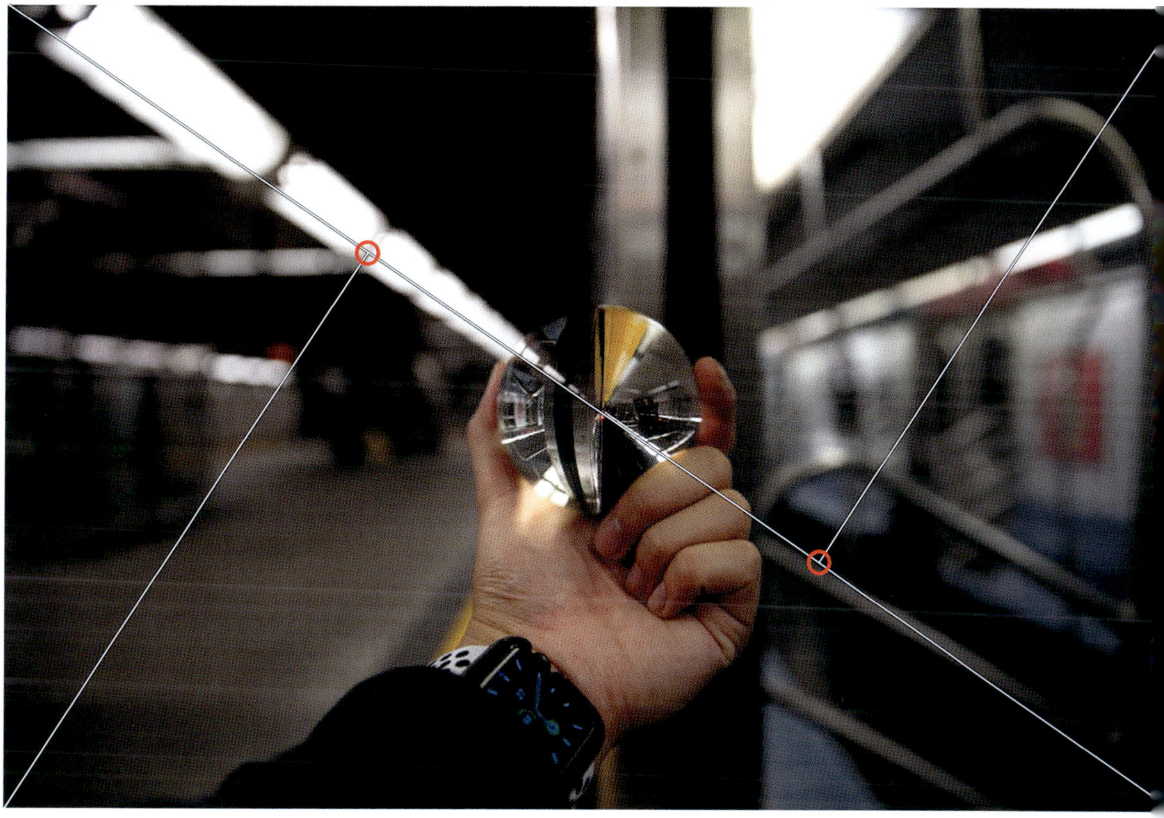

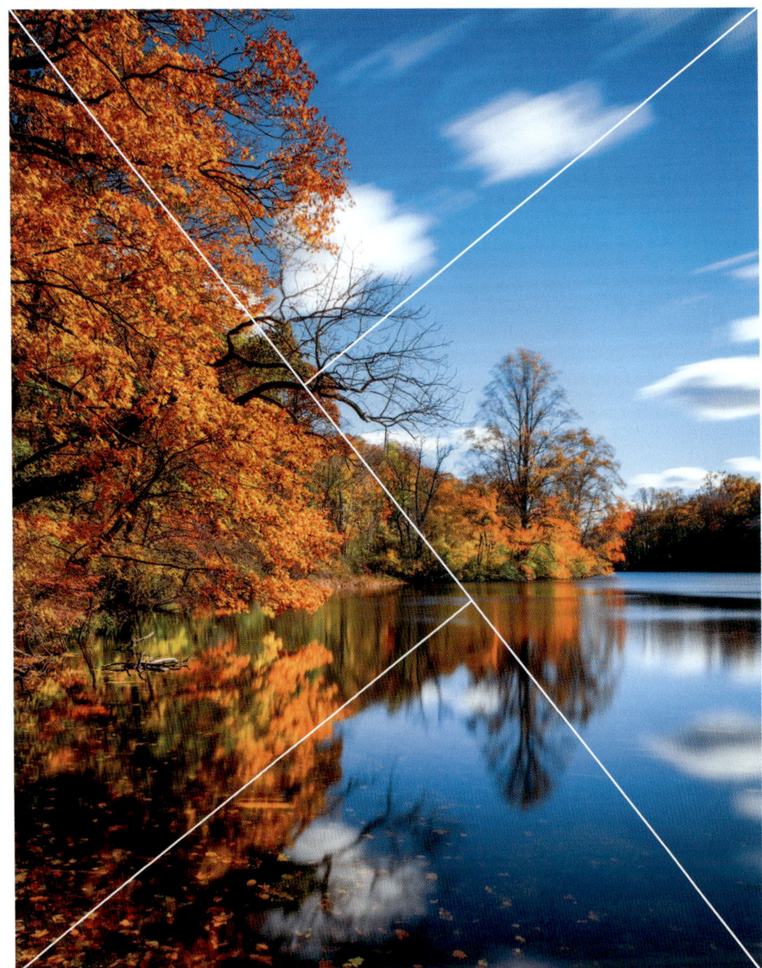

Golden Spiral

The composition method known as the golden spiral is probably the most interesting of the ones discussed in this chapter, as its measurements are based on the Fibonacci Sequence, where each number is the sum of its two preceding numbers:

0, 1, 1, 2, 3, 5, 8, 13, 21, 34, and so on...

The golden spiral and the rule of thirds are very similar in that the end of the spiral typically meets with one of the four intersections (figures

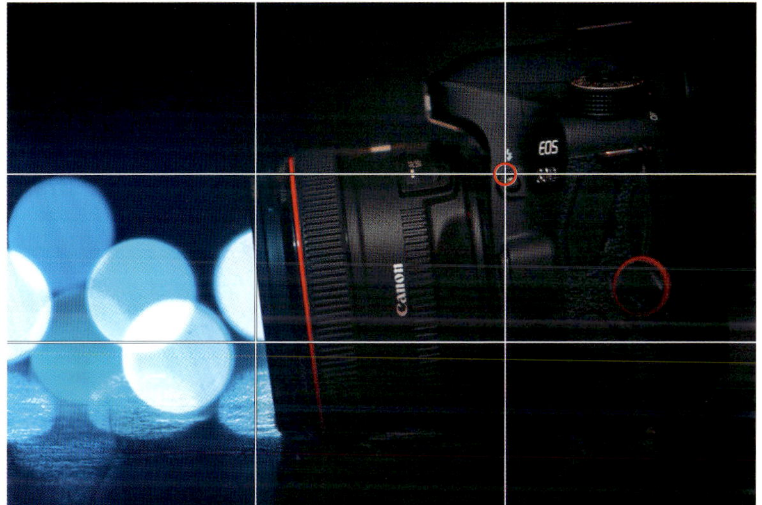

Figure 5.9a

185mm | F/2.8 | 1s | ISO 50

A photo of my Canon 70D taken halfway across the room with a 70–200mm lens. The blue lights in the background are amber fairy lights that I cooled down to blue in post-processing. I've applied the rule of thirds grid to the image, where the point of interest is the model number of the camera and the highlights and shadows reside in their separate zones.

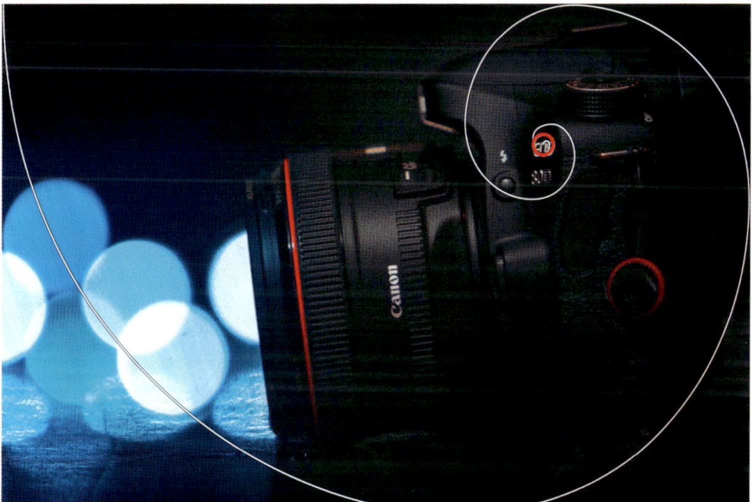

Figure 5.9b

The same image of my camera overlaid with the golden spiral to illustrate how similar the two composition methods can be.

5.9a and 5.9b). This, however, does not mean they are interchangeable. There are characteristics of both that make them work with unique, individual photos. The golden spiral usually fits well when there is a curved leading line from the corner of the image (figure 5.10). I don't generally set up lensball photos according to the golden spiral, but I may notice certain photos are pleasing to the eye and find out afterward that they follow that concept.

Figure 5.10

24mm | F/16 | 15s | ISO 100

Curved leading lines such as coastlines, or in this case light bokehs, can direct the viewer through the golden spiral to the point of focus, which can be the tip of the light bulb.

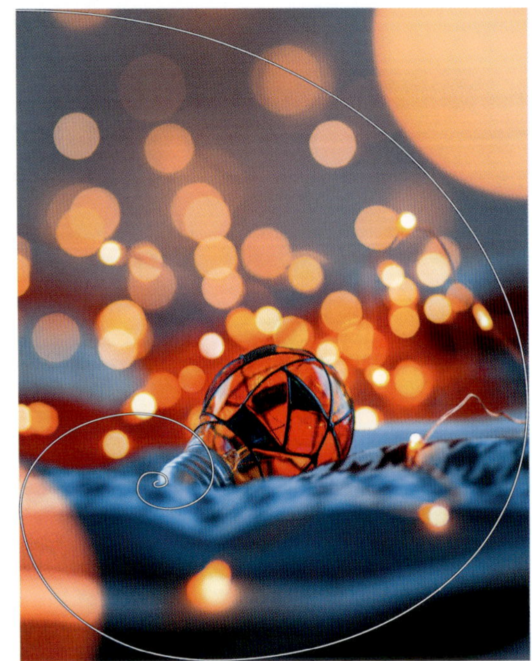

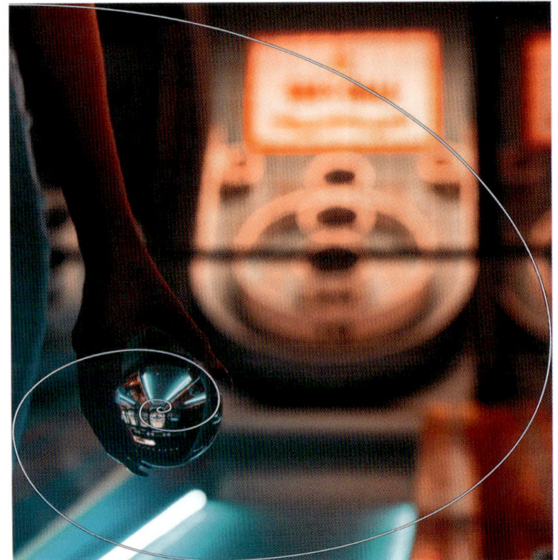

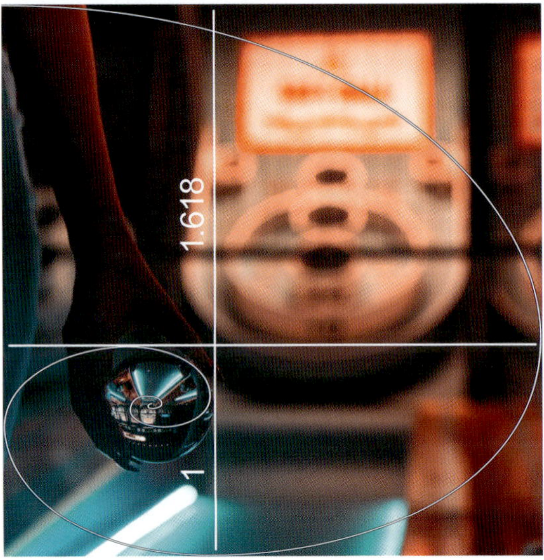

Figure 5.11a

85mm | F/4.0 | 1/250s | ISO 2000

The golden spiral is overlayed onto a lensball image that was taken in front of a skee-ball machine, with the lensball held by my friend Danielle.

Figure 5.11b

The golden spiral, or ratio, can also be used to separate an image into two sections where the midline is skewed by a ratio of 1 to 1.618. The smaller half will have the subject still in the middle of the spiral. You can tell if you have successfully composed this by removing the larger half from the top portion and noting whether the image is still acceptable.

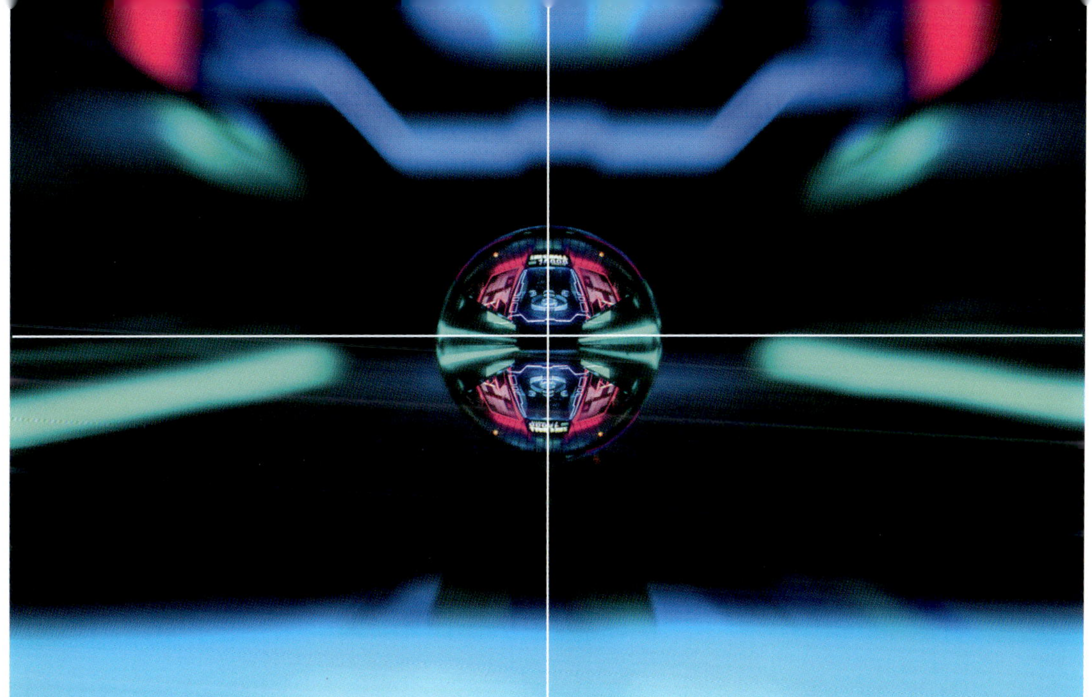

Center Composition and Symmetry

Many will argue that simply placing subjects directly in the middle of the frame may make the image boring, but center composition can still lead to a visually appealing photo if done intentionally. I tend to shoot a significant amount of my lensball photos with center composition and symmetry in mind. The ball itself is a perfectly symmetrical object, so why not put it directly in the middle. This compositional method works best when there are reflections and symmetrical balance within the framing. A lot of times you will find that things like puddles and lakes help drastically for this type of composition.

Leading Lines

Leading lines are described as lines in an image that are intentionally used to frame a subject or guide the audience toward a specific point. This is one of the strongest and most apparent compositional tools that you can use in your photographs. I use this technique in the majority of my lensball photos because it provides an obvious visual guide for the viewer. There are many different types of leading lines that can be used in photography, but for my work I focus on three: horizontal lines, diagonal lines, and converging lines.

Figure 5.12

67mm | F/2.8 | 1/125s | ISO 100

Center composition works best with a balanced top and bottom or balanced left and right section. In this capture of another lensball on a skee-ball machine, symmetry exists on both the left and right sides of the background, as well as on the top and bottom within the lensball.

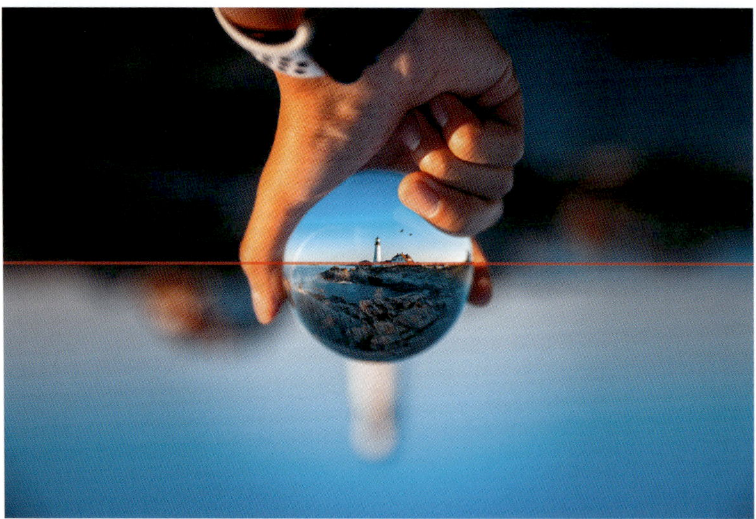

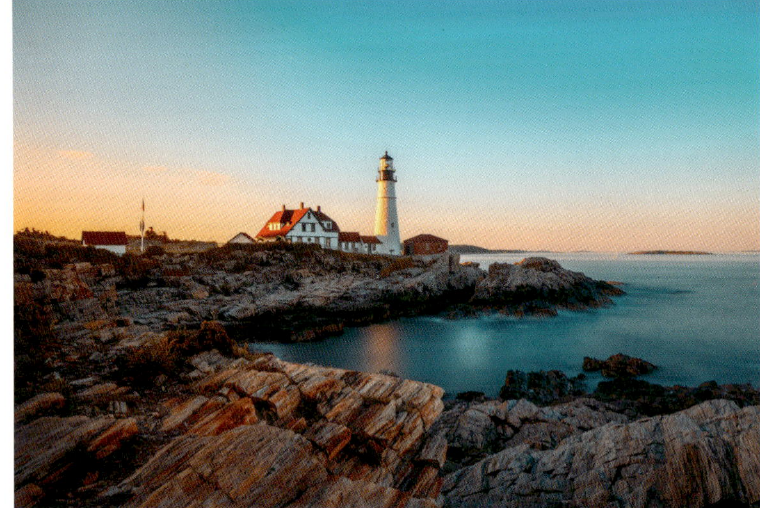

Horizontal Lines

Horizontal lines exist almost everywhere with oceans, bridges, and buildings. The use of these lines helps strengthen the composition and provides stability to the overall image. A great way to utilize this in your lensball photos is to align the horizontal line within the ball so that it bleeds into the horizontal line of your backdrop. This anchor is an excellent way to provide guidance for those who struggle with composition.

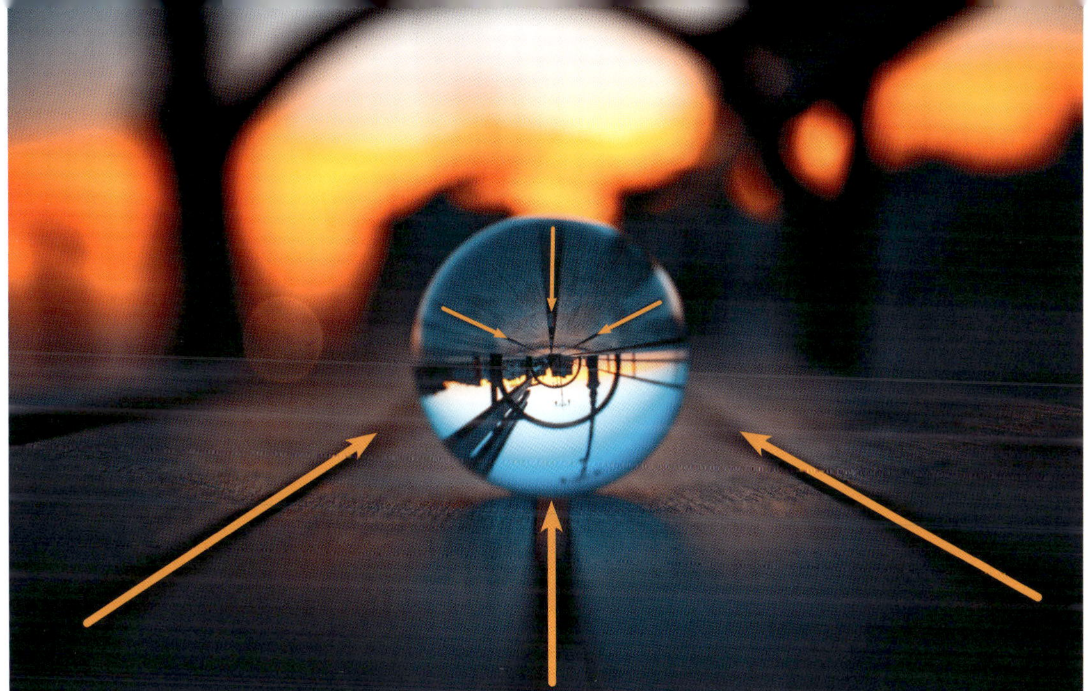

Diagonal Lines

Diagonal lines are meant to create depth for an image. Although they are somewhat unbalanced, they can help draw the viewer's eyes into the photo. A best practice is to set the lines from one side of the image toward the subject. It is very popular to use this when trying to emphasize distance within a frame. Because our eyes naturally pan left to right, this tactic can guide the audience between foreground and background fairly effortlessly.

Converging Lines

Similar to diagonals, these lines also add depth to the image. Things like railroad tracks, stairs, and bookshelves can be useful additions when trying to bring attention to something at the intersection. Because this is such a strong compositional element, it is important to align the subject at the axis of the two converging lines when framing the shot. One unique thing about shooting through a transparent object like a lensball is that you can situate the converging lines inside the glass with the lines in the background.

Figure 5.14

70mm | F/2.8 | 1/125s | ISO 100

This image was captured on a park bench outside of Coney Island. The gaps in between the planks of wood act as diagonal leading lines pointing in toward the image inside the lensball. The purpose of these lines is to create a feeling of depth in the two-dimensional image.

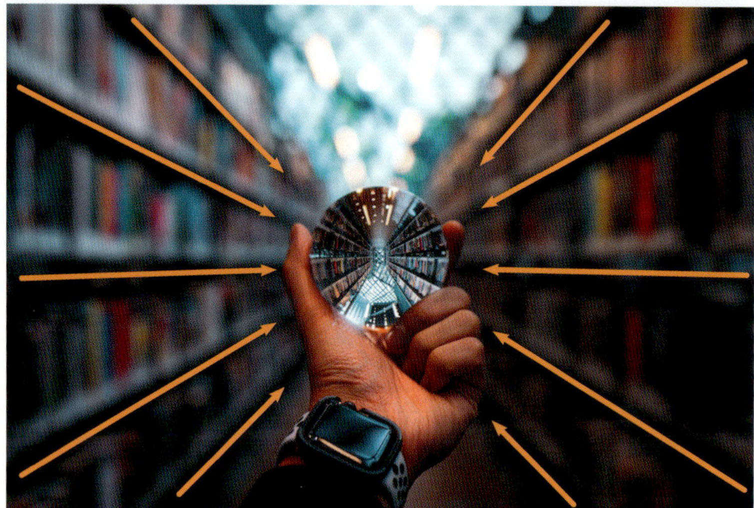

Patterns

Unlike the previous compositional tactics, the use of patterns does not require leading lines to make your image captivating. Patterns exist almost everywhere and it is your job as a photographer to discover them. They are basically repeating elements in the background that grab the viewer's attention if used correctly. What's interesting about this technique is that when shooting with a lensball, you must also be conscious about how the pattern will appear within the ball. Because

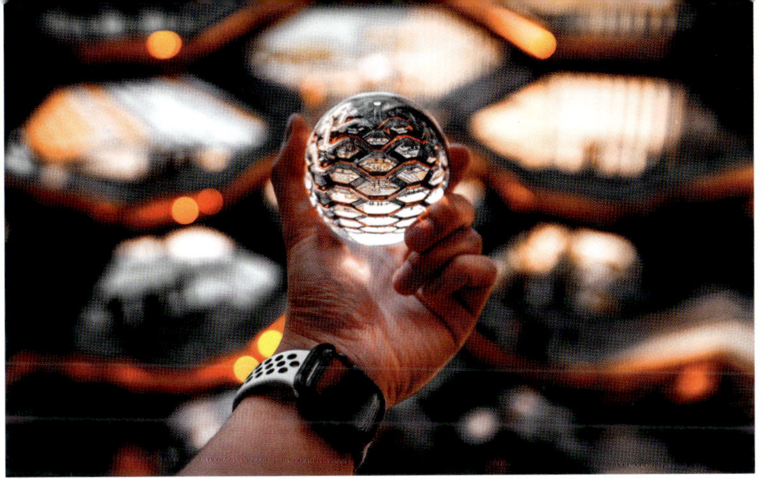

Figure 5.16

35mm | F/2.8 | 1/1000s | ISO 100

Although the repeating pattern does cover the backdrop, the lensball has some open space near the inside of the hand. This particular shot was taken on top of the Vessel in New York City.

the lensball acts as a super-wide-angle lens, your pattern might fill the frame of your camera's backdrop, but the image in the lensball might not wrap far enough to fill the secondary frame.

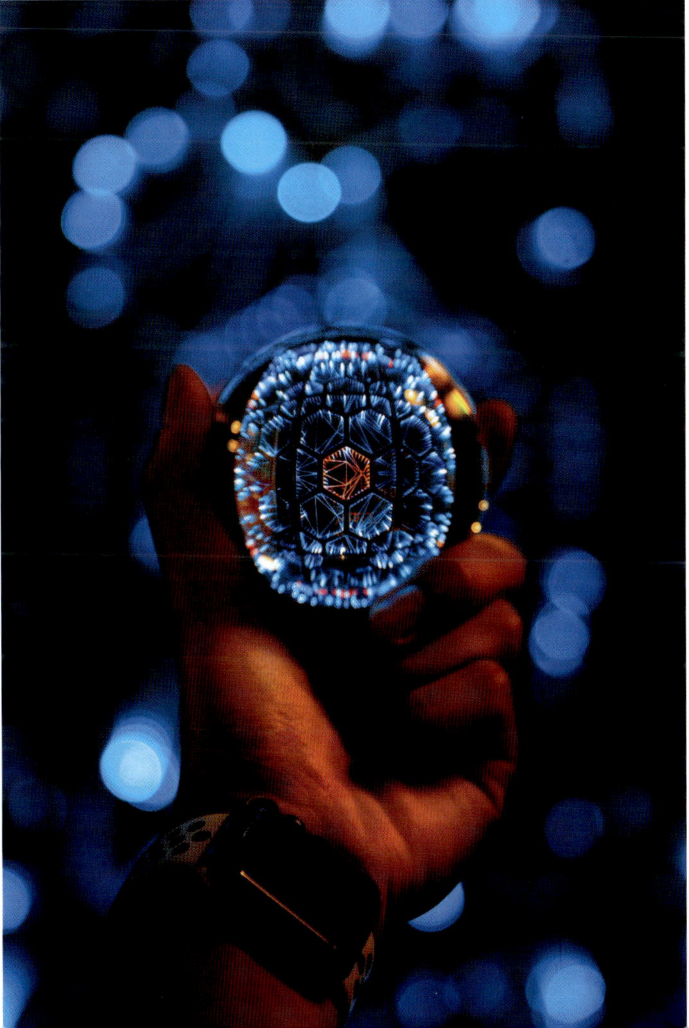

Figure 5.17

70mm | F/2.8 | 1/160s | ISO 800

This was taken in front of an LCD screen that displayed repeating hexagonal patterns. This can also be replicated with a television or large monitor.

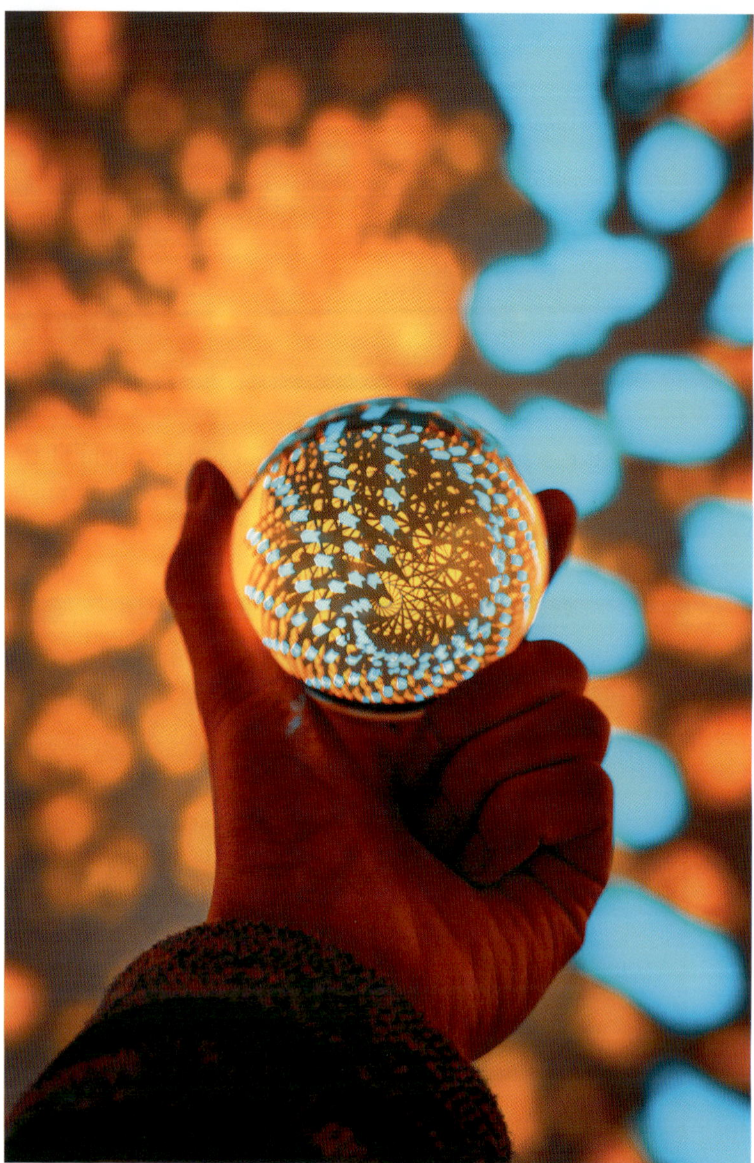

One of the drawbacks of shooting indoors is that most of your lensball photos will be backlit, which will leave your hand in the shadows.

As mentioned before, you must encompass both a good composition
within the lensball as well as around it. My favorite practice is to shoot
with a slightly telephoto lens to develop a final image that includes
both a compressed and wide composition.

CHAPTER 6

Creating your Canvas

One of the most popular themes for lensball captures is incorporating natural landscapes. There are many different colors and compositions that exist in the wild and it's up to you as the photographer to use them meticulously. There are three components that matter the most to me when shooting outdoors, two of which we've already discussed: color contrast and composition. The third, which we'll discuss in this chapter, is lighting.

Understanding how light works when building an image is the most important job of any photographer. Without light, there will be no photo. In terms of natural light, the use of sunlight will affect your images differently depending on the time of day you shoot. I could go into an entire tutorial just to discuss the different avenues of natural light, but for this guide I will condense it down to four types: hard and direct light, dappled light, diffused light, and reflected light.

Direct Light

Hard and direct light is what you would typically see on a cloudless day around noontime. This type of light is great if you want images with high contrast and defined highlights and shadows. This is the most difficult light to work with in terms of shooting a lensball because the quality of light is very harsh. You may have difficulty capturing colors or getting proper reflections in your lensball. Your camera also may not have a wide enough dynamic range to take in all the detail within the shot. The highlights may be washed out or details can be lost in the shadows.

Many photographers find this direct light uninspiring and will shoot at an earlier or later time of day. During this lighting condition, you will find me capturing shots under trees or in shaded areas since that type of light better fits my style. If you are stuck shooting with harsh lighting, try to position the sun behind you so that the backdrop in front of you is properly lit.

This image was captured in front of Machu Picchu around noontime, when the sun was the strongest. The difference between the highlights and shadows is fairly apparent. It is difficult to balance out the contrast even in post-production.

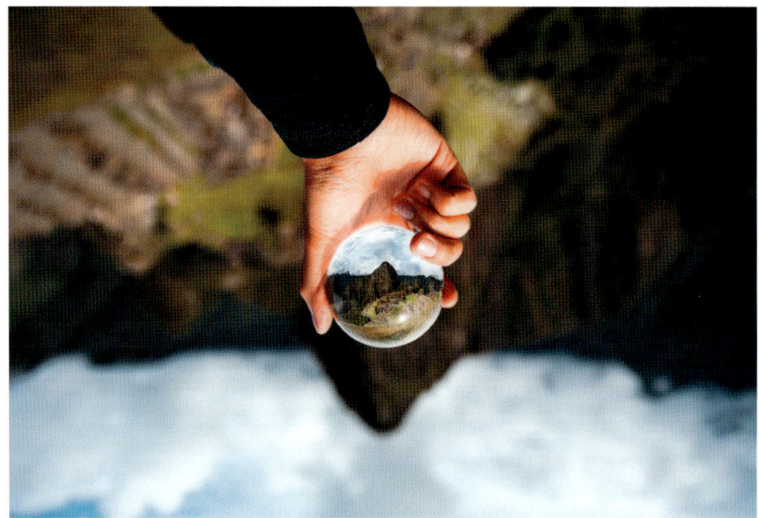

One thing to take note of is that you may want to use wider lenses when shooting in direct light. Because shadows are more pronounced under midday sun, you can obtain a more interesting backdrop when using a focal length under 50mm. Also, be wary that the lensball functions just as well as a magnifying glass and might burn your hand under direct sunlight!

You can use the bright sunlight to your advantage to create strong contrast with the bright reflections and shadows. This can help make your image seem more vibrant and eye-catching. For this shot, I used a mini tripod to elevate the ball so it wasn't submerged in the pond, and I was able to achieve a clear lensball reflection in camera.

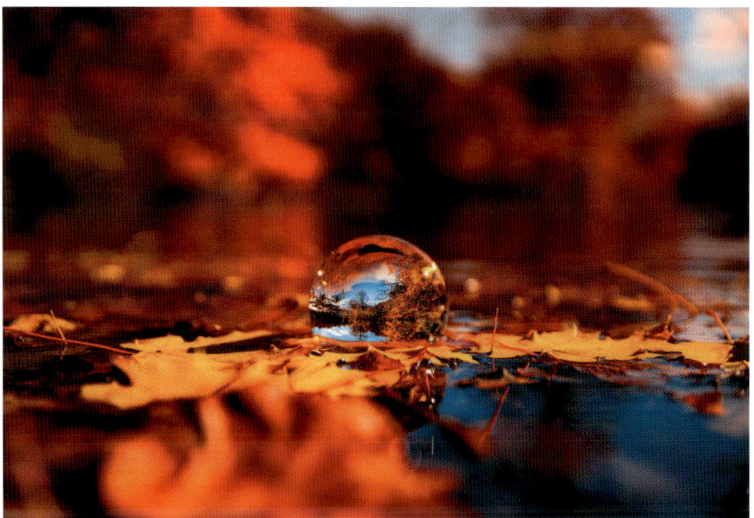

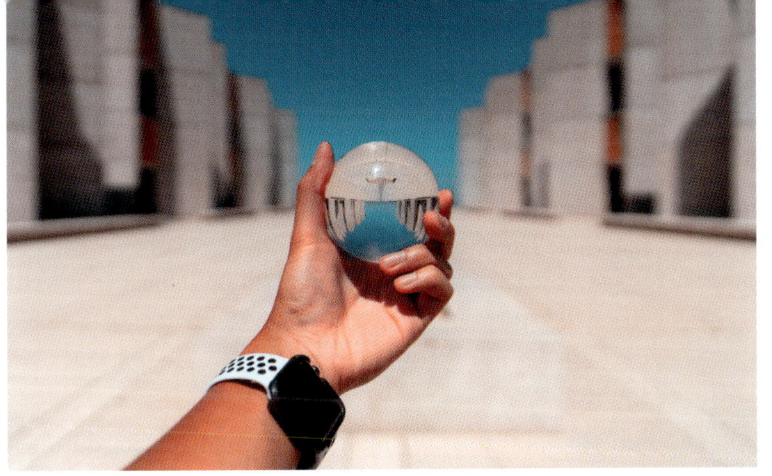

Figure 6.3

24mm | F/2.8 | 1/8000s | ISO 100
This is an example of how shooting in harsh, direct light can drain out the interest in a scene. On location, it was difficult to hold the lensball up to the camera, as the sun would burn my hand if exposed for too long. Also, the lack of gradient in the sky and shadows on the ground left the image feeling two-dimensional.

Dappled Light

Dappled light is sunlight that has been filtered through the leaves of trees or other plants. This effect usually works best in the morning or late afternoon. This can be a hit or miss if you are a portrait photographer, as unwanted hot spots can appear on your subject's face during the shoot. However, for lensball photos I really enjoy using the scattered light as my backdrop, especially during the fall and spring when the sun travels at a lower angle in the sky. When photographing a scene with trees or flowers, you will notice that the colors of the leaves and petals are accentuated and give the image an overall better color contrast (figure 6.4). In the summertime, the strong light tends to wash everything out and drains out most of the interest in the photo.

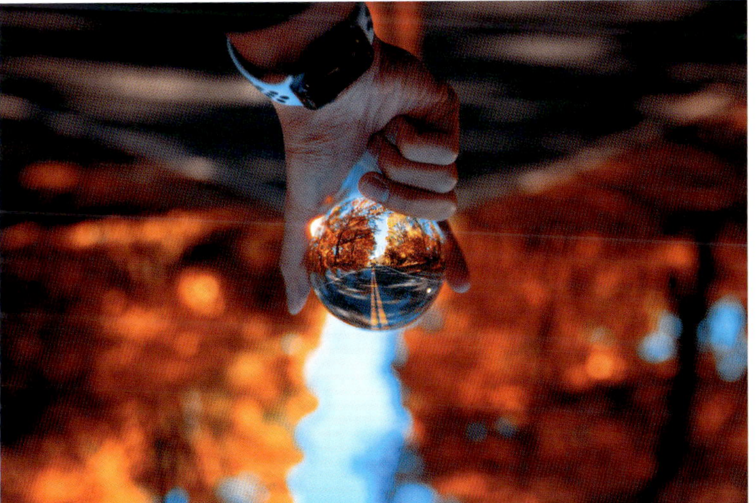

Figure 6.4

35mm | F/2.8 | 1/400s | ISO 100
Experiment with shooting under a canopy of trees to capture a high color contrast. This can be done either midday or during low sun.

The distance between the ball and a dappled light backdrop will affect how scattered the highlights are in the photo. The one challenge you will face in this lighting situation is metering the image appropriately. Your in-camera metering may pick up the scattered highlights and shadows individually, which can cause underexposure or overexposure, respectively. I try to align the lensball or subject in a well-balanced area and expose for that accordingly.

Diffused Light

Soft and diffused light is usually found on a cloudy day or during a sunrise or sunset. It is great if you are looking for mild shadows and blended edges. This lighting scenario is ideal if you want an overall flat image for more control during post-processing.

During these situations, I focus on compositional elements rather than color contrast to build my framing (figure 6.5). Some locations to look out for with overcast weather are places with a lot of trees or moving water. Leaves, bark, and branches create subtle contrasts that can work in your favor (figure 6.6a). Things like waterfalls and long-exposure seascapes appear smooth and well exposed in this lighting. Do not get discouraged from shooting just because it is a cloudy day. There are always unique photos you can capture, and practicing will only make you that much better of a photographer.

Figure 6.5

35mm | F/2.8 | 1/250s | ISO 100
Take advantage of an unsaturated scene to focus on monochromatic photos. Use the available architecture and landscape elements to enhance your photo in a diffused-light setting.

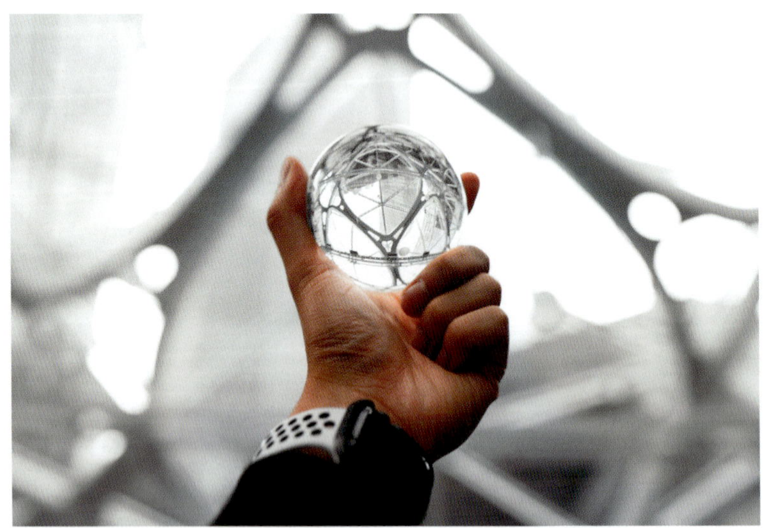

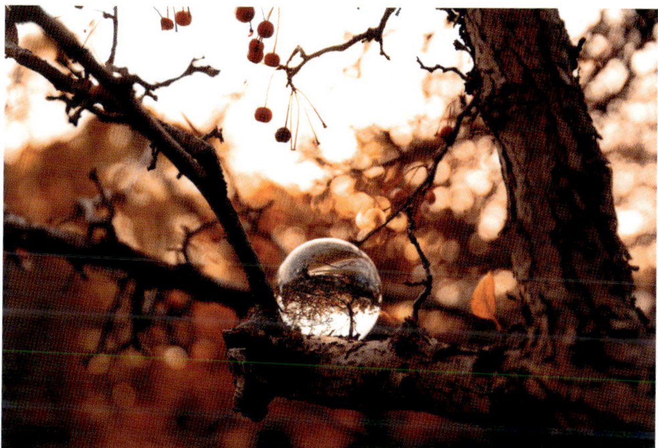

Figure 6.6a

50mm | F/2.8 | 1/250s | ISO 100

Placing the lensball on branches will exemplify the minute textures in the wood, as they are both in the same focus plane. Angling the branch down toward camera-right allows for a nice falloff in the photo.

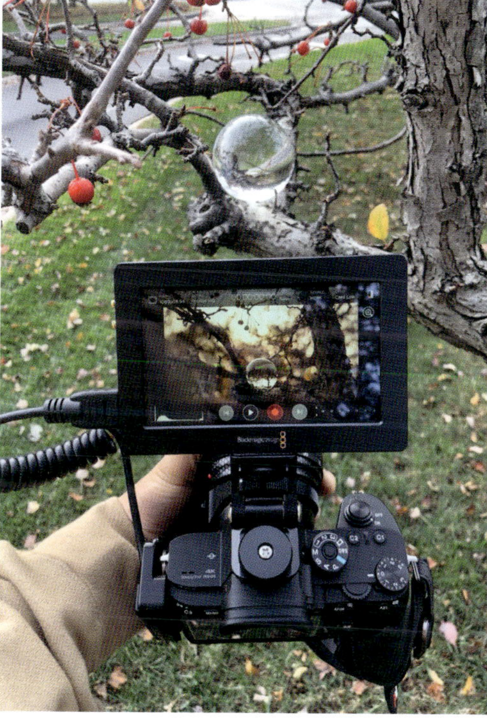

Figure 6.6b

Using an external monitor can help you frame an image without being at the mercy of your camera's flip screen or viewfinder.

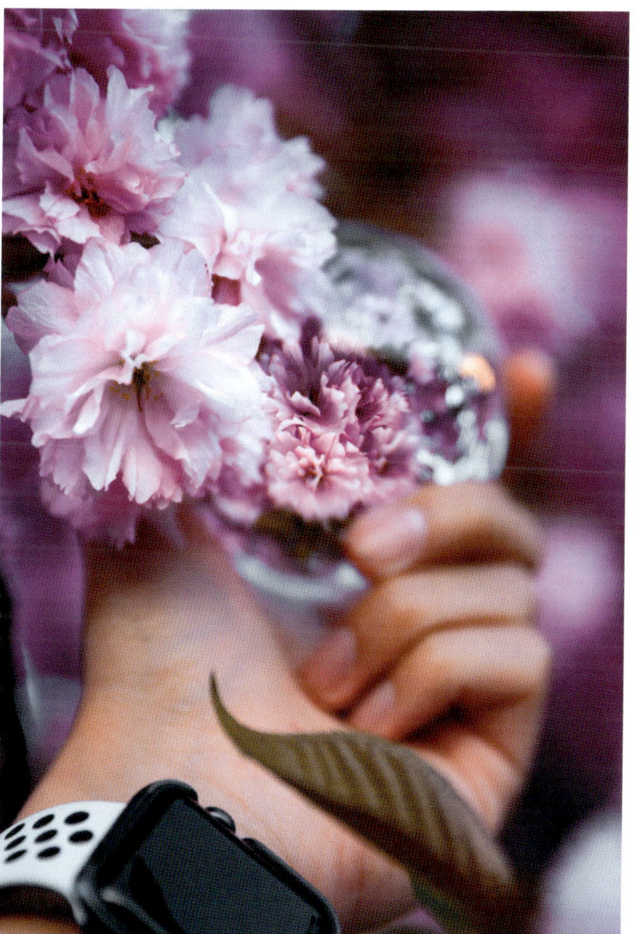

Figure 6.7

70mm | F/2.8 | 1/160s | ISO 100

The soft tones in this image are primarily the result of diffused lighting. There are no abrupt separations of color, which allows the overall image to seem coherent.

Reflected Light

Lastly, my favorite lighting condition is reflected light. This is described as a soft color cast or the glow from light bouncing off objects. Reflected light will affect your image differently depending on what type of surface it hits. Light bouncing off grass will have a different feel than light reflecting off of water. Harsh reflected light can add brilliant colors to your lensball photos. This can be produced by placing the lensball in water or on reflective surfaces. I honestly feel this is where the product shines, and I have seen many photographers compose really creative images with this lighting scenario. The natural in-camera contrast you obtain in these photos will make it much easier to bring out colors when editing.

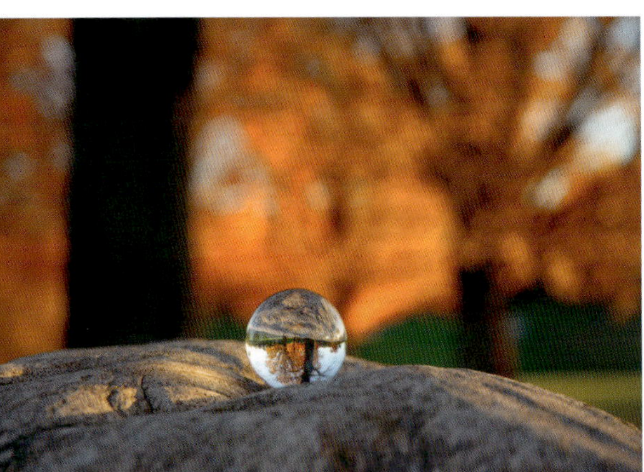

Figure 6.8a

70mm | F/2.8 | 1/250s | ISO 100

In this image, reflected light is bounced off the boulder and autumn leaves for a soft color contrast. The photo was captured an hour before sunset at a nearby park. Shooting at eye level with the ball will provide you with sharp details in the rock while compressing the background.

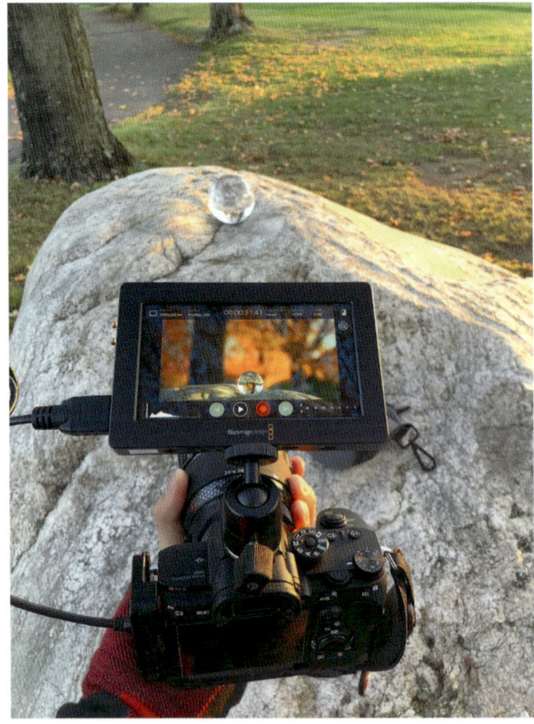

Figure 6.8b

This is a behind-the-scenes capture of figure 6.8a. Leveling the ball and camera at the same height will create a large distance between the foreground (rock) and background (trees) for strong subject separation.

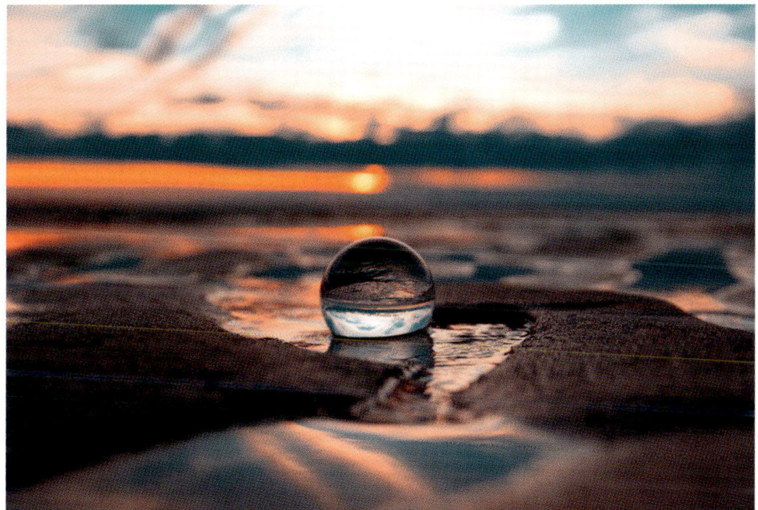

Figure 6.9a

33mm | F/2.8 | 1/800s | ISO 100
Sunsets can add beautiful colors into reflective surfaces like still water. This is most apparent on semi-cloudy days because you need the sunlight to bounce off the clouds to contrast the blue in the sky.

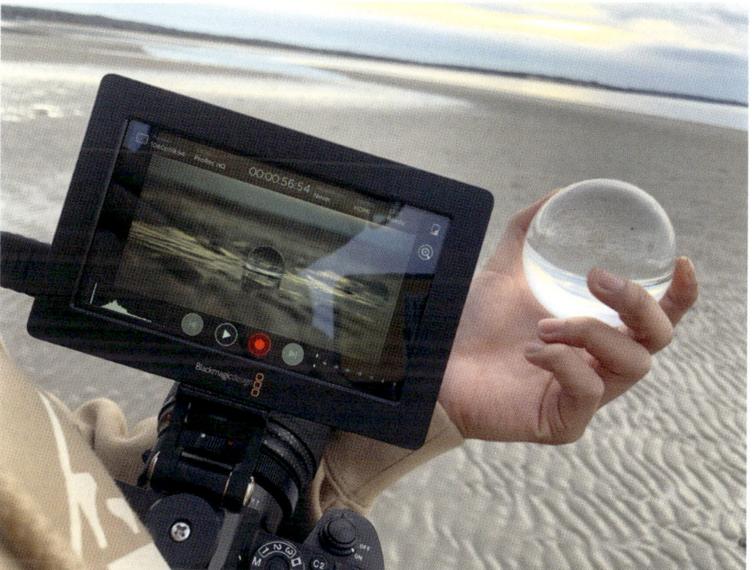

Figure 6.9b
A behind-the-scenes shot to illustrate how a boring location can make for a great image.

Figures 6.10a–6.10d illustrate how reflected light affects your images based on the focal length at which you shoot. You will notice that as you use more telephoto lenses, the lighting in the back becomes softer and loses contrast. The photographs shot at 24mm (figure 6.10a) and 35mm (figure 6.10b) appear more vibrant because the light bounces off more surfaces. The images shot at 50mm (figure 6.10c) and 70mm

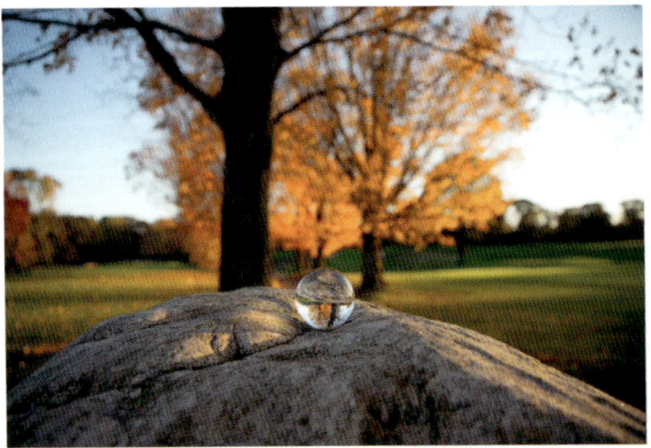

Figure 6.10a

24mm

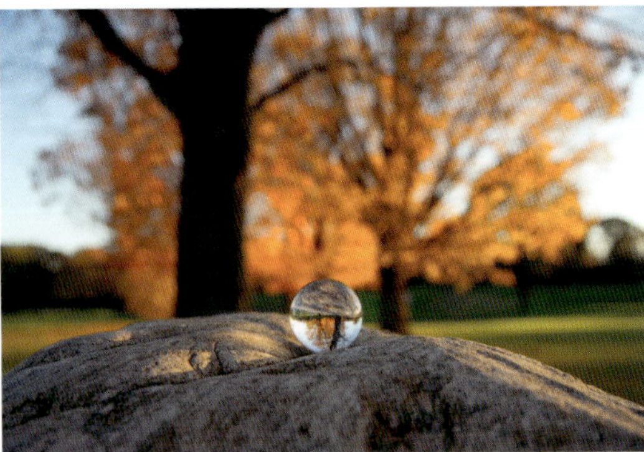

Figure 6.10b

35mm

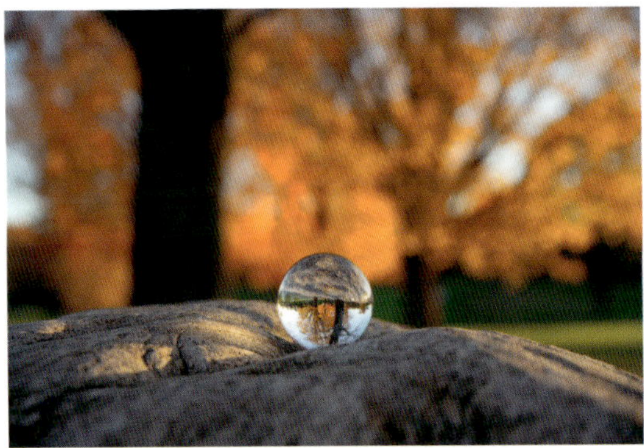

Figure 6.10c

50mm

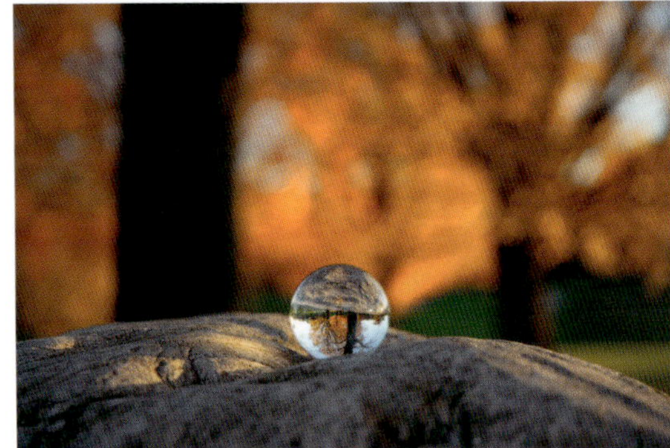

Figure 6.10d

70mm

(figure 6.10d) showcase more of the light reflected from the tree leaves and less from the grass.

Overall, there really isn't ever "bad" lighting in nature; rather, it is whether or not the light works for your vision.

Capturing a City

When it comes to putting compositional theories into practice, urban areas are a great training ground to hone in your craft. Cities are packed with rigid lines and defined architecture, which work really well with lensball photography. My main goal for shooting in urban environments is to look for elements that give my shots more of an impact. For me, these photos concentrate less on color and more on contrast and composition.

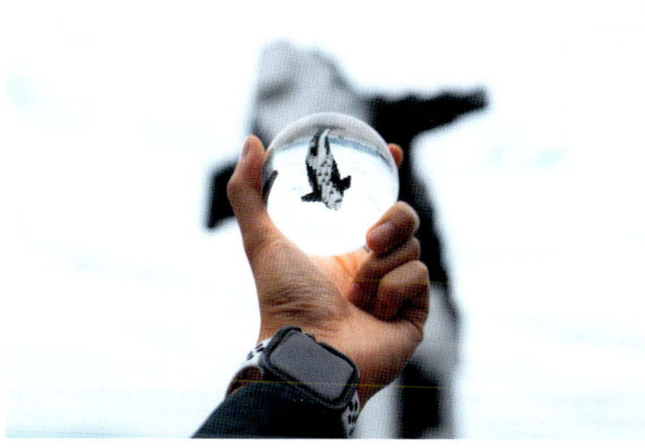

Figure 6.11a

35mm | F/2.8 | 1/1600s | ISO 100

A capture of the *Digital Orca* from Vancouver. I always thought it looked neat, regardless of whether it would work well in a lensball photo. I had to shoot upward toward the sculpture to remove the ground within the lensball.

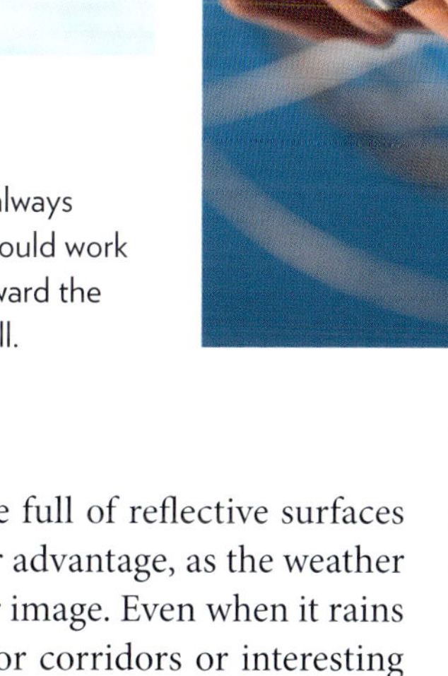

Figure 6.11b

24mm | F/2.8 | 1/3200s | ISO 100

Circular sculptures like the *Unisphere* in Flushing Meadows Corona Park can act as both framing elements as well as fitting subjects for lensball images. In this image, the globe in the background frames the lensball, which then frames the globe within.

Unlike with a scenic nature shot, cities are full of reflective surfaces and artificial light. You can use this to your advantage, as the weather has less of an effect on the outcome of your image. Even when it rains you can find buildings with unique interior corridors or interesting lighting setups. In addition, puddles can be a huge benefactor when you're looking to spice up a photo. Puddles on concrete or metal help create a better mirrorlike reflection than they do in a natural setting such as on sand or mud. The reason for this is that the puddle is generally more controlled in an urban environment and there will be fewer ripples or shifting in the water. I'm not saying you should be placing your lensball in random puddles in the city, but you can take a strategic approach and carry a bottle of water with you to create your own puddles. The more prepared you are, the better control you have of the environment.

Take your time to research the different monuments and building structures in the city you want to visit. You can take some really awesome lensball photos where you "capture" famous landmarks in the ball (figures 6.11a and 6.11b).

Lighting is just as important for urban shots as it is for nature photography, and it will heavily influence your photos depending on the time of day as well as weather conditions. This is especially important when you're photographing locations with tall buildings or reflective surfaces. The sun will cast shadows at different angles in the morning, midday, and evening times, which will affect the overall lighting contrast within the lensball. Whenever I travel to the city, I like to take notes of when certain locations have the best light, while also noting the direction and strength of light. This is especially handy when planning out different captures, as portrait and landscape photography prefer different qualities of light.

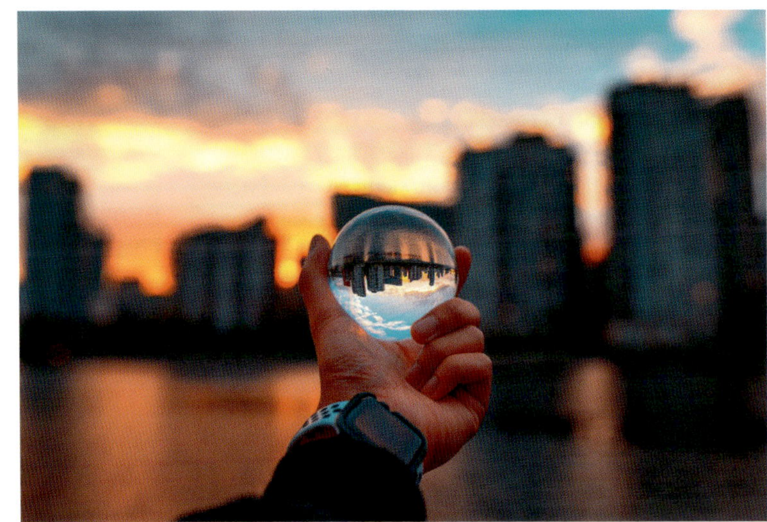

Figure 6.12
35mm | F/2.8 | 1/320s | ISO 100
Try to plan your location in advance based on where the sun will be during the specific time you want to shoot. I have a few apps I use to track the sun, but the weather app built into the iPhone works just as well.

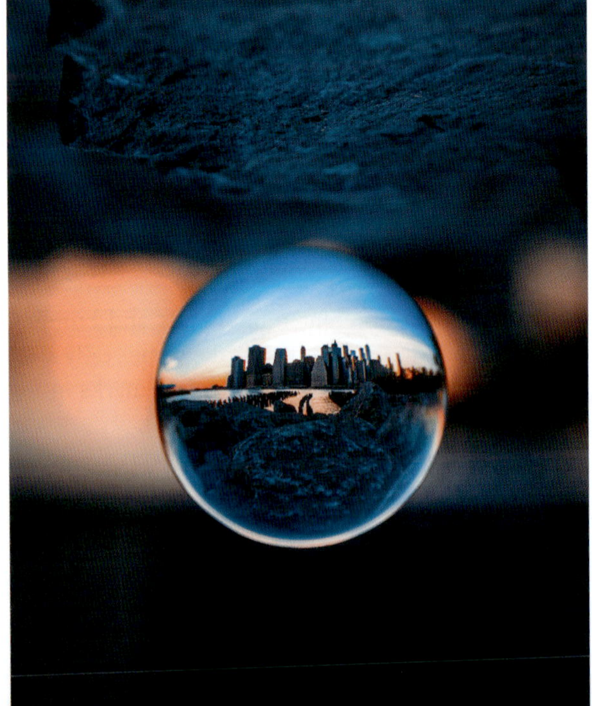

Figure 6.13
70mm | F/2.8 | 1/100s | ISO 100
A capture of the Manhattan skyline through a lensball. I waited a little too long to shoot and the sun passed the horizon, giving this more of a silhouette look. The floating effect was created by using the lensball stand and then removing it in post-processing.

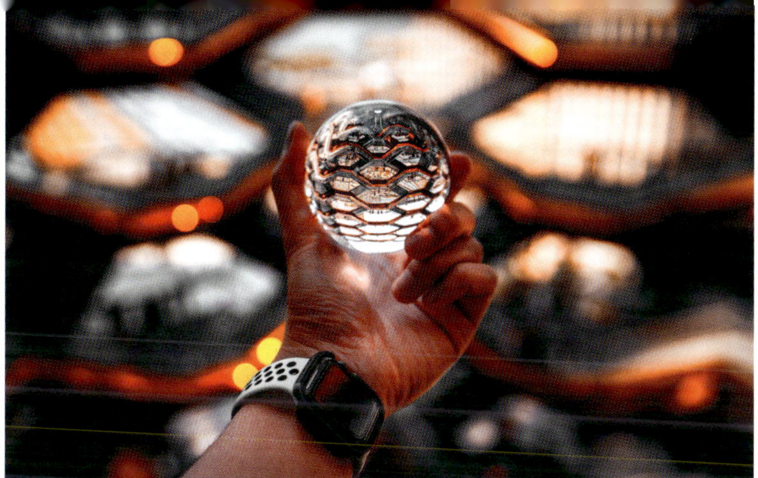

Figure 6.14 was captured at the Vessel in New York City. A wider-angle lens was used to incorporate the repeating pattern in the background instead of leaving it too compressed. Shooting this at my usual 70mm focal length would have not left enough breathing room for the ball. To acquire a full pattern within the lensball, I had to aim it down because I was near the top of the structure. Shooting this leveled would have led to more of the white sky bleeding in from the bottom of the sphere. Even though this was shot at a wider focal length, because there was a good amount of distance between the ball and the background, it still produced a shallow-depth-of-field look. The lighting in this shot was reflective, as I relied on the sun to bounce off the metal structure to create a high-contrast image. The shot was taken midday to early afternoon, which helped draw out the defined highlights and shadows. I would have liked to have captured it with the sunset, but during this season the sunset was eclipsed by an adjacent building after five o'clock.

Capturing iconic structures like the Manhattan Bridge within a lensball makes the shot stand out more than a two-dimensional image of just the bridge as your subject (figure 6.15b). Figure 6.15a was taken on a cloudy afternoon in Dumbo, Brooklyn, under diffused lighting. The overcast weather gave the photo an even, flat light throughout the scene. I used a telephoto focal length for this capture to bring out more detail from within the ball. Shooting at 50mm or lower would have weakened the separation between the ball and the bridge and allowed further distractions from the surroundings to creep into the image. Be sure to visit these locations at off-peak times to avoid tourists. Although I visited during a weekday, I still had to Photoshop a few people out of the lensball.

Figure 6.15a
70mm | F/2.8 | 1/320s | ISO 100

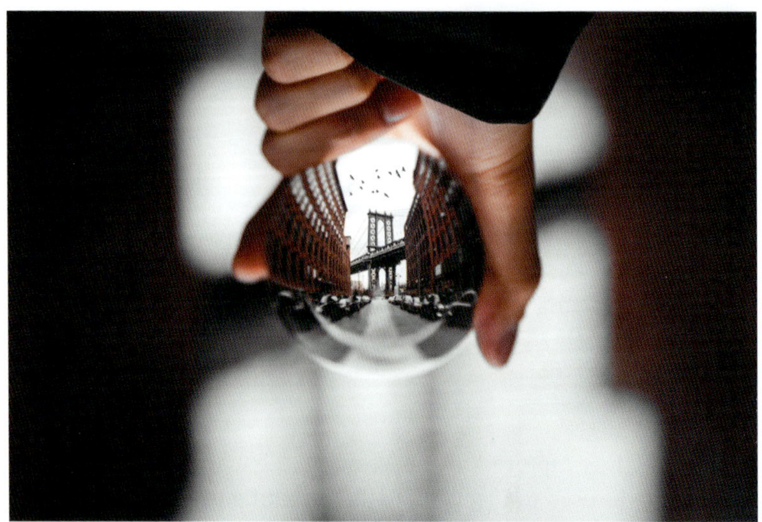

Figure 6.15b
24mm | F/22 | 1/160s | ISO 800

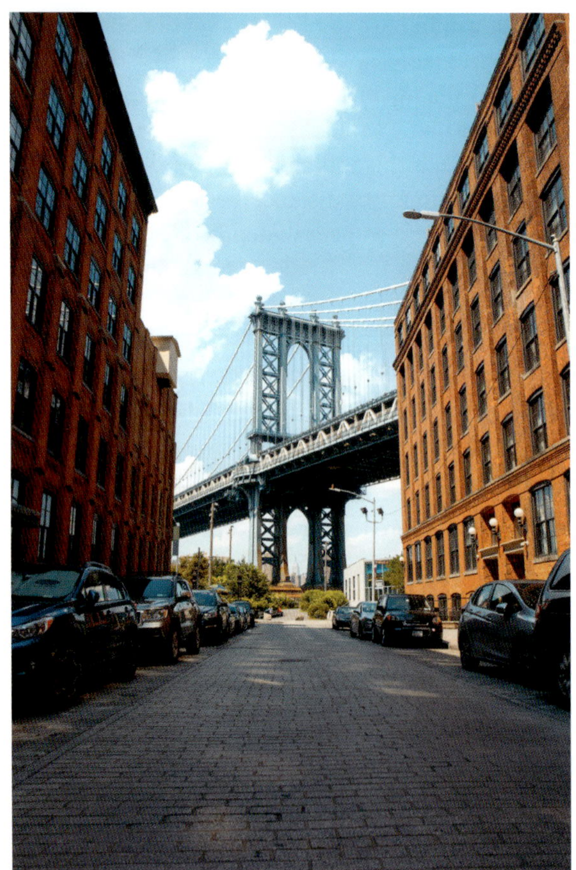

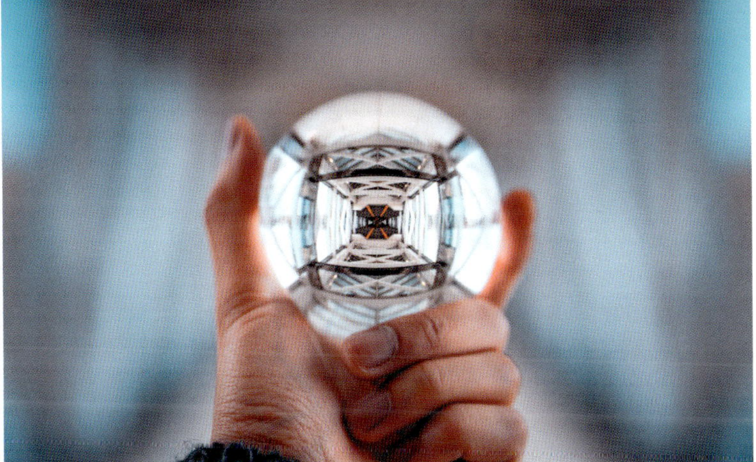

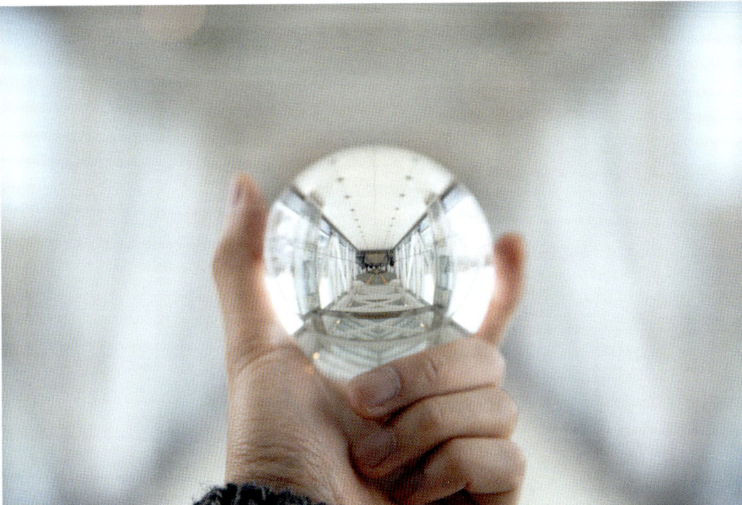

Long hallways and corridors are excellent for defining leading lines in your shot. Be sure to stand directly in the middle and align the lensball so that the lines of the background lead into that of the foreground. Since the ball reflection and the background work inversely, any slight movement can throw you off alignment. I captured figure 6.16a on a bridge that connected two parts of a mall together. I focused on aligning the ceiling and floor edges with the compressed bokeh lines in the back to create cohesive leading lines between the two compositions. I then edited the inside of the ball to incorporate a flipped ceiling, as it was more interesting to look at than the floor (figure 6.16b).

Architectural elements such as ceilings can be great compositional tools. Be sure to look up next time you enter a tall building or structure to see if you can find anything unique to capture. You may be surprised that simple things like windows and stairways can become a main subject for your lensball photos. I would advise using a wide-angle lens for these types of images to capture more of the environment. As mentioned earlier in this chapter, circular backdrops create a unique frame for these types of captures (figures 6.17 and 6.18). Square and rectangular backdrops may not be as interesting, but it is always worth trying them out (figure 6.19).

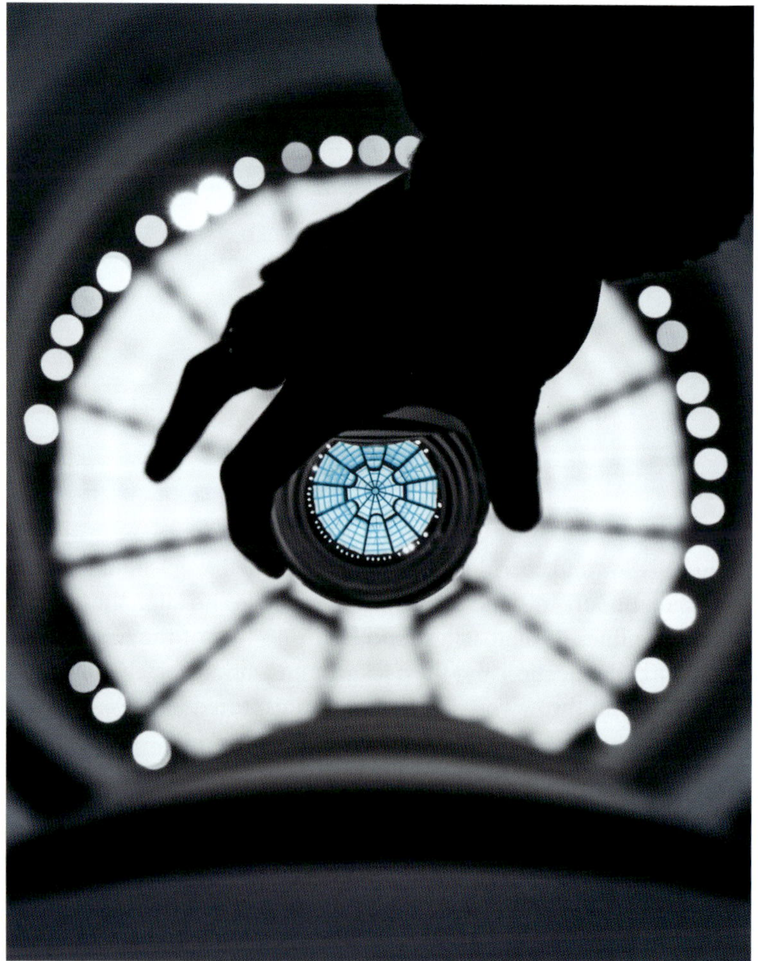

Figure 6.17
24mm | F/2.8 | 1/60s | ISO 100
I captured this image by aligning the lensball with the glass ceiling of the Guggenheim museum in New York.

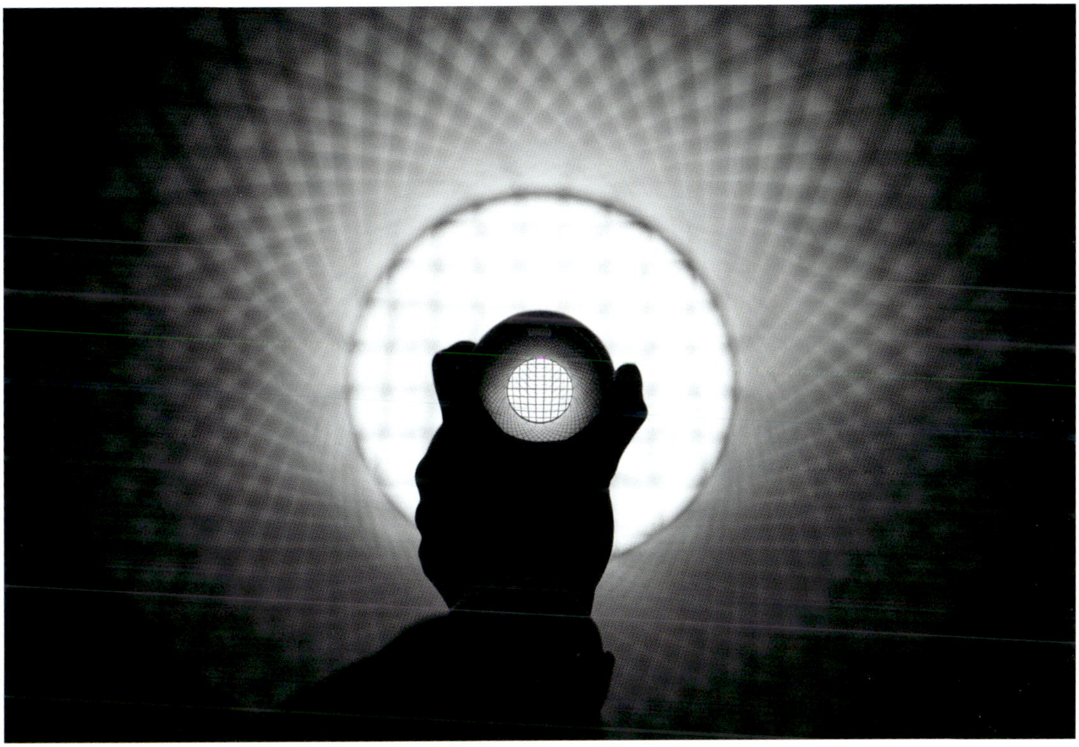

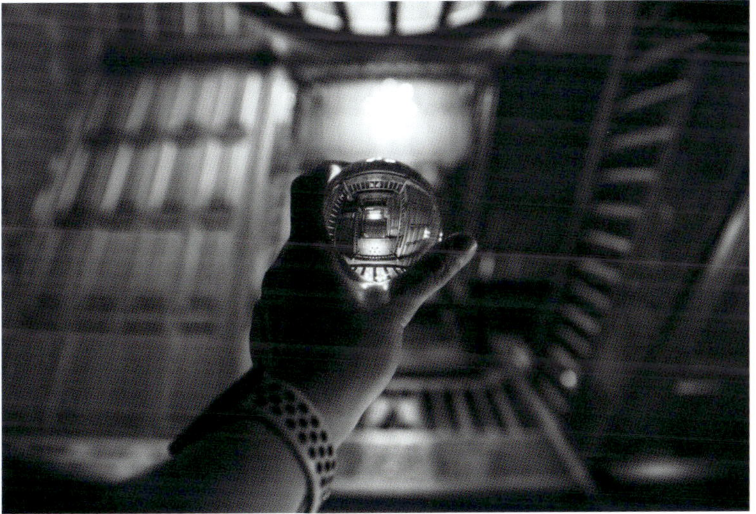

Figure 6.18

24mm | F/2.8 | 1/250s | ISO 100

To create the composition for this image, I stood directly underneath the Fulton Street subway station ceiling.

Figure 6.19

24mm | F/2.8 | 1/125s | ISO 1600

An example of utilizing stairways to frame a shot. I edited this as a monochromatic image to exemplify the compositional details.

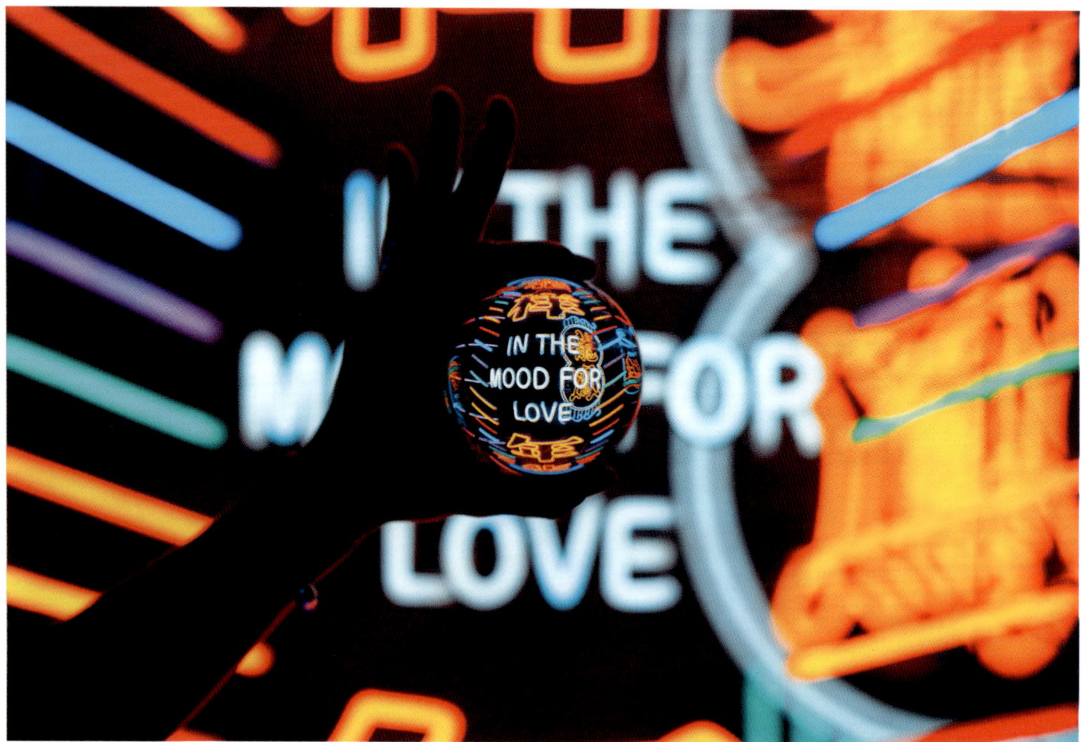

Figure 6.20

I shot this image in front of a neon sign at an art exhibit in Manhattan. Because I was using an 85mm telephoto prime lens, I had my fiancé, Nicole, hold up the ball for me, as the minimum focusing distance was longer than my arm. I flipped the projection inside the lensball during post-production because I wanted the words to align with the backdrop.

Lastly, neon and LED lights can be used as strong subjects and backgrounds. Although lights are not tied specifically to the city, you will find they are more common in the streets or inside art exhibits. The best time to capture these scenes outside would be immediately after sunset. Capturing lights can also work during the nighttime, but you run the risk of the environment being too dark and introducing motion blur if you're shooting with Auto or Aperture-priority settings (figure 6.22). It is easier to darken a properly exposed image than brighten an underexposed one. You can also find a good amount of colorful lights in arcades and at carnivals.

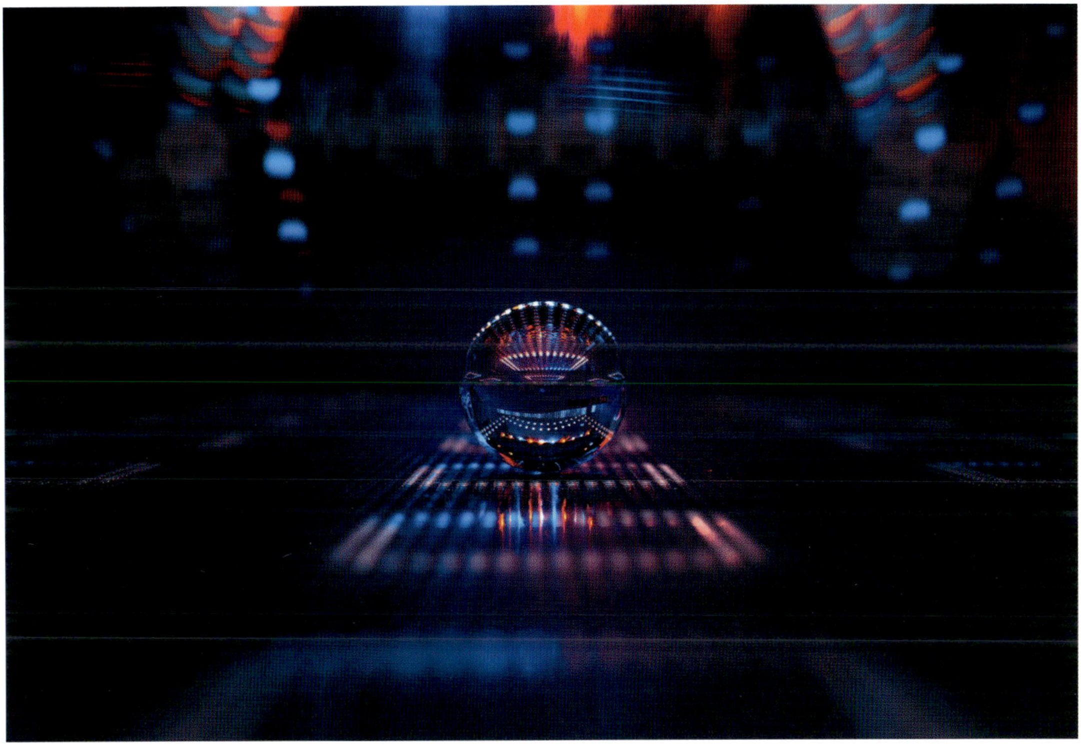

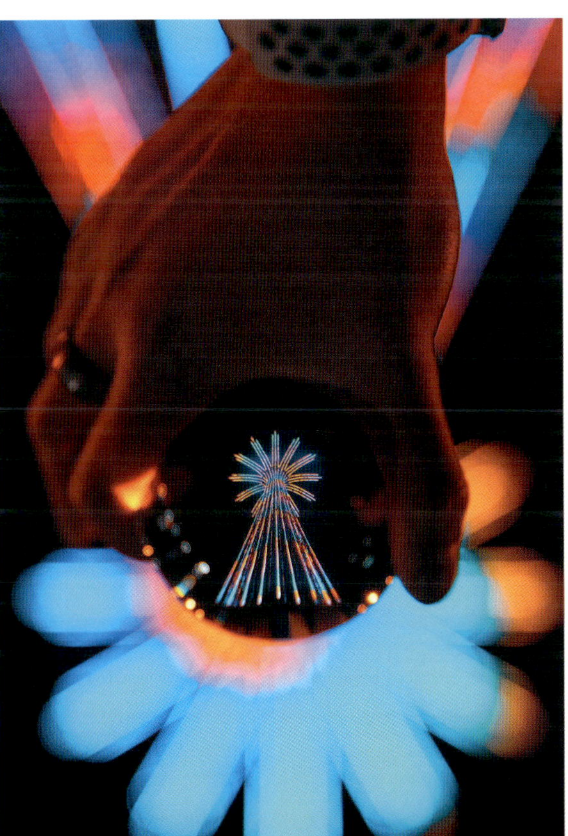

Figure 6.21

50mm | F/2.8 | 1/100s | ISO 100

For this photo, I placed the lensball over an interactive LED panel at a Sony pop-up exhibit in the city. I used a triangular glass prism to reflect the light pattern from the back to help frame the image.

Figure 6.22

50mm | F/2.8 | 1/80s | ISO 800

I took this photo at Coney Island Park in Brooklyn, New York. It was way past sunset and there was limited lighting to maintain a balanced exposure between my hand and the background. I also had to increase my ISO and drop my shutter speed to get a decent shot.

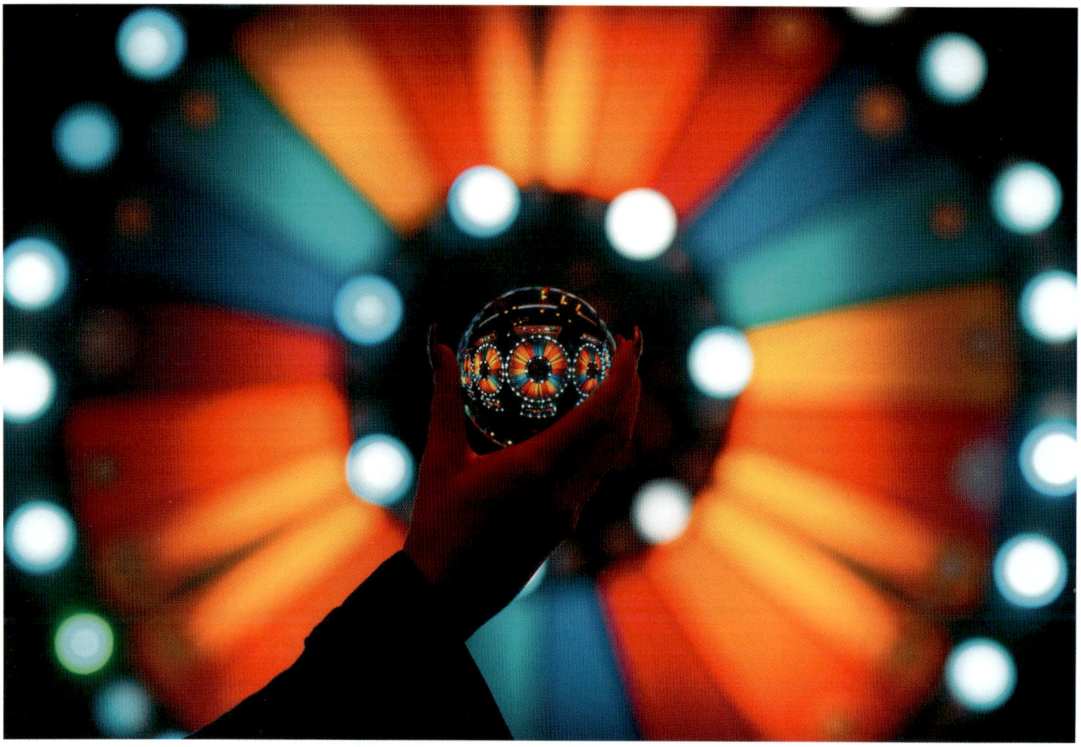

Figure 6.23

85mm | F/2.8 | 1/250s | ISO 640

Find ways to use lighting to frame the shot. Not every photo needs to have the main focus inside the lensball. I took this photo at a local arcade near my house, with the lensball held up by my friend Danielle.

Figure 6.24

85mm | F/2.8 | 1/250s | ISO 4000

For this image, I positioned the lensball on the ledge between two Pac-Man machines. The ISO was pumped up to 4000 to maintain a high shutter speed so that motion blur would not be apparent in the final image.

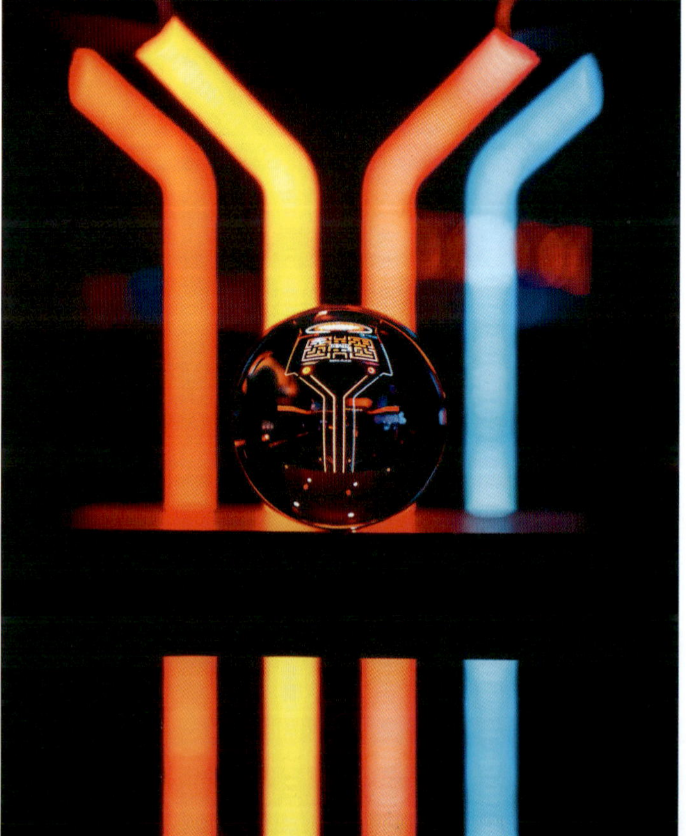

CHAPTER 7

Post-Processing

In this chapter, I'll cover the methods I use when post-processing my lensball images. Each photo I take is edited slightly differently since no shot is the same. I know it is popular to use presets, but they may not work with every lighting or color-combination scenario. Mastering your own editing process will be beneficial in the long run, as you will gain an understanding of how certain techniques and adjustments work for your captures. I primarily use Adobe Lightroom Classic for raw color manipulation. As of this writing, there are two versions available—Lightroom CC and Classic—the only difference being that CC is more of a cloud-based application while Classic is primarily for a local workstation or laptop that includes all of the functionality. I only bring my captures over to Photoshop if I want to add additional elements or remove distractions.

For those who have never used Lightroom or a similar editing software, it may seem daunting with so many settings and visual graphs to look through. I'll go over some of the common tools I use that can also be found in other free editing software like GIMP and Pixlr. However, one thing I do enjoy about Lightroom is that the changes

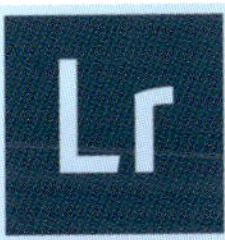
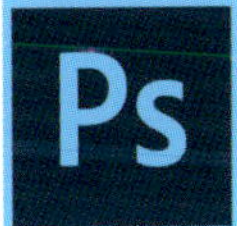

Figure 7.1
Adobe Lightroom Classic
Workspace

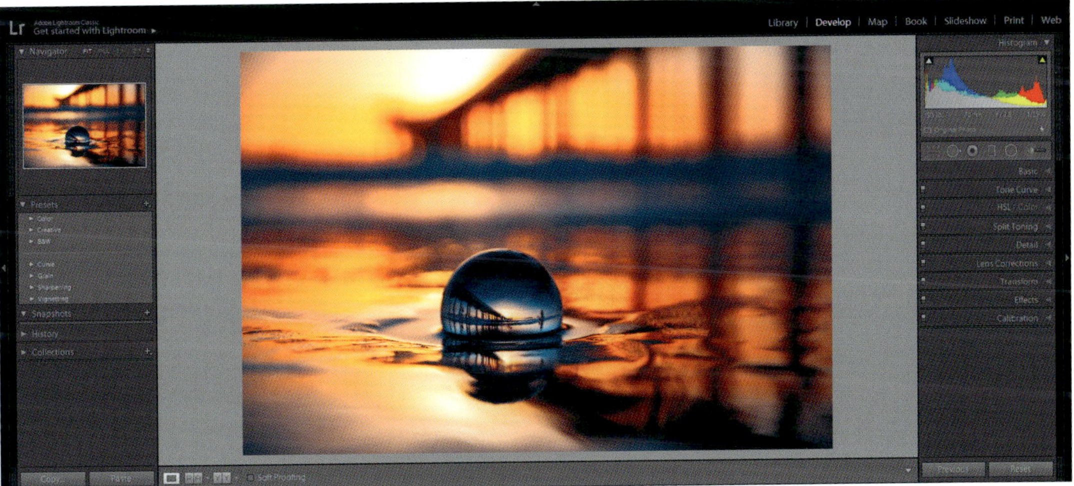

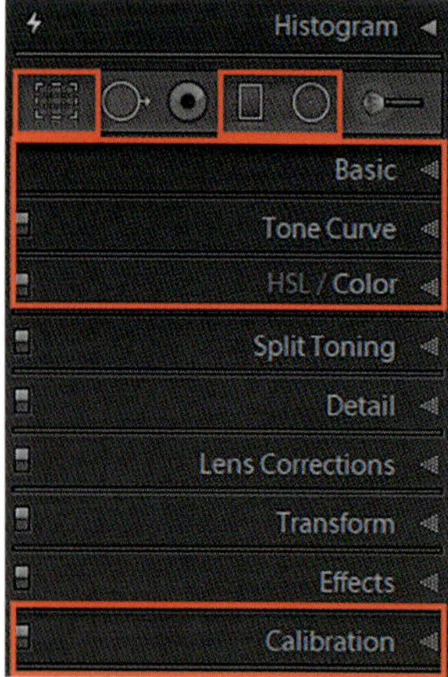

Figure 7.2
General settings

Figure 7.3
Cropping, aspect ratio, and straightening

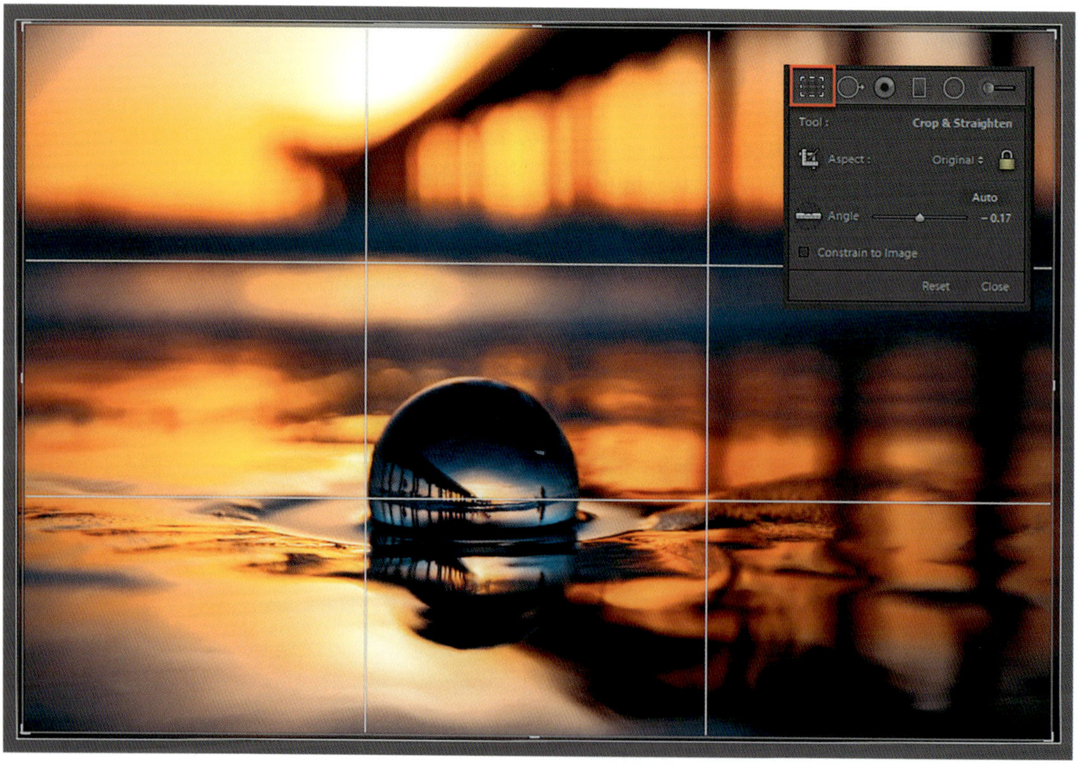

made are nondestructive, meaning the original image file is not modified. Unlike Photoshop, where saving an image will overwrite the existing file, Lightroom creates a file with all the edits and overlays it on the raw picture.

Note: I will be explaining the setting changes with a Windows keyboard in mind. This is great if you ever need to revert any modifications or just want to start over.

To keep my workflow simple, I really only use the settings outlined in figure 7.2 when I'm editing any lensball photos. In this chapter, I'll break down the functionality of the tools and how I incorporate them into my editing process.

Crop Overlay

Setting the correct crop and angle alignment should be the first adjustment you make to an image when post-processing. The cropping tool is one of the few functions you can use on an image to set

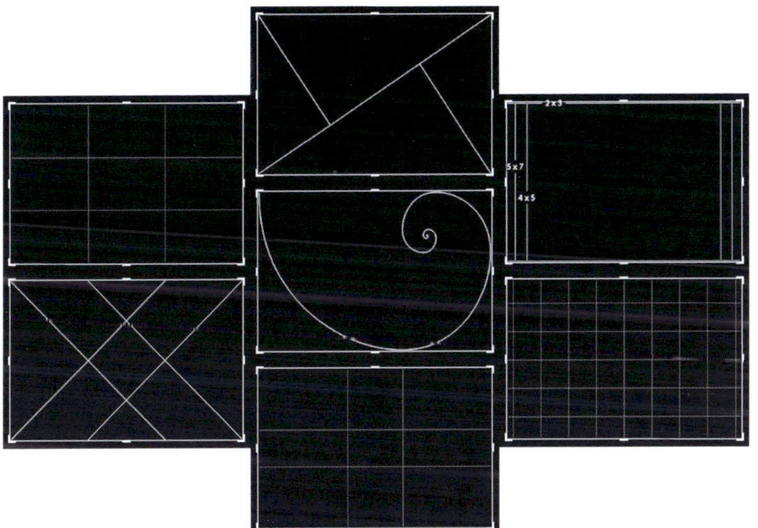

Figure 7.4
Each of these overlays can
be toggled by pressing O on
your keyboard. Holding down
the Shift key and pressing O
will allow you to rotate the
guides.

the overall story and composition. I try my best to acquire the final look of the picture in camera, but there are times where I notice minor distracting elements near the edge of the frame or need to reposition the subject in post.

My first step is typically to figure out the composition I want for the photo. As explained in chapter 5, there are a number of compositional guides you can follow to position subjects in the frame. The same is true after the fact when you have the ability to crop or adjust the aspect ratio of the image. Lightroom has a set of built-in overlays you can toggle through to see which guide works best for your photo (figure 7.4).

The next step I take is to align the horizon as flat as I can in the image. Unless you've intentionally tilted the image to create an interesting composition, a crooked photo can give the audience a sense of imbalance when viewing your work. This is even more apparent when you print your art to be displayed in a gallery or office. The straightening tool is a quick fix for future headaches (figure 7.5).

The aspect ratio is another setting I adjust only after all of my other settings have been dialed in. The reason behind this is I want to make all the changes I need to on as much of the image as possible. Setting the aspect ratio is a fairly easy change and is dependent on the outlet where I am sharing the picture.

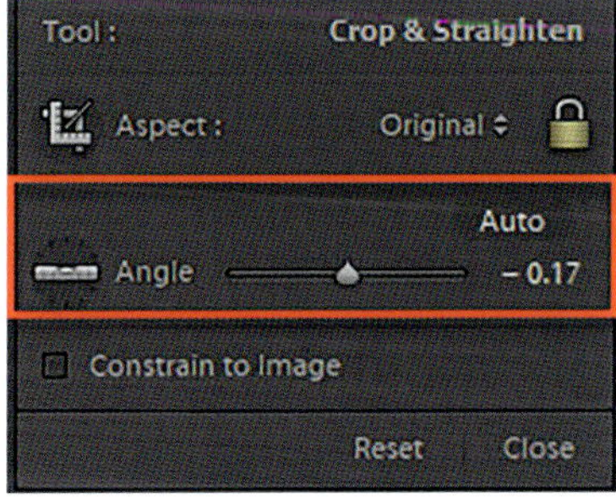

Figure 7.5
There are three tools you
can use to straighten your
image. If you click on Auto,
Lightroom will make an
assumption of where the horizon should be. The Leveling
icon will allow you to drag a
line across the image, and the
image will rotate according
to that horizon. For a more
precise measurement, you
can enter in the number of
degrees by which the image
will rotate.

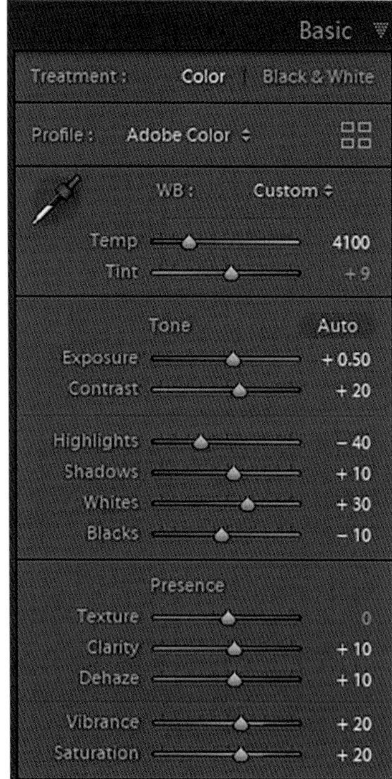

Figure 7.6
The Basic panel

Basic Adjustments

After the general crop has been set, I make minor changes with the toolset in the Basic panel (figure 7.6). I try to shoot most of my images slightly underexposed and only need to bump the Exposure up by around +0.5. For Contrast, I try not to go overboard and I limit it at +20. Any higher and you will start losing details in the shadows and highlights.

The Highlights, Shadows, Whites, and Blacks sliders are fairly self-explanatory. I try to balance out the image to maintain the details I want to keep. Dragging the highlights down will allow you to see things that would have been lost due to overexposure. Bringing up the shadows can recover details you lost from underexposure.

In the Presence section, I change it up depending on how I want the overall image to look. Most of my photos utilize up to a +10 Clarity and +20 Saturation, which gives them a crisp yet colorful look. Try to keep these settings as conservative as you can in the beginning, and come back to them once you finish making the other changes.

Tone Curve

The Tone Curve is potentially the most powerful tool when it comes to post-processing. Although it may look complicated, there are a few adjustments you can keep in mind to achieve your desired edit. The Tone Curve simply represents the exposure of the overall image in a continuous line. Going from left to right, the curve starts with the shadows, then moves the midtones, and ends with the highlights (figure 7.7a). Moving parts of the curve upward will make the corresponding areas of the image brighter, and dragging it down will make them darker.

For this step, I usually add two points for the shadows and highlights by clicking on the line, and drag them slightly down and up, respectively, to add a subtle contrast. This is commonly known as an "S" curve because the shape of the curve resembles the letter. When doing this I try to maintain the midpoint relatively close to where it started out. If the image is too dark after those adjustments, I will place a third point for the midtones and drag it up slightly to brighten up the overall image. In some of my darker images, I will drag the leftmost

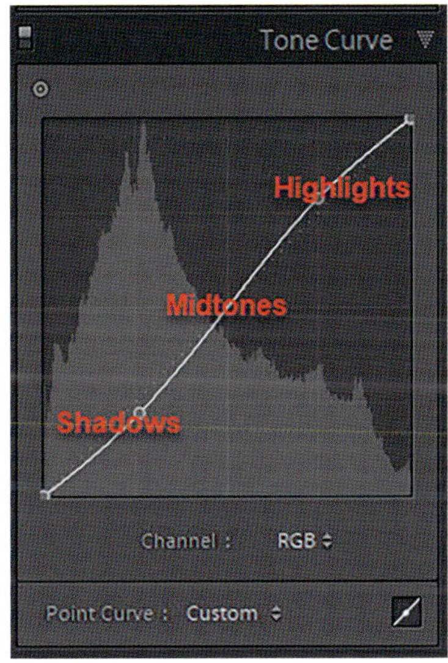

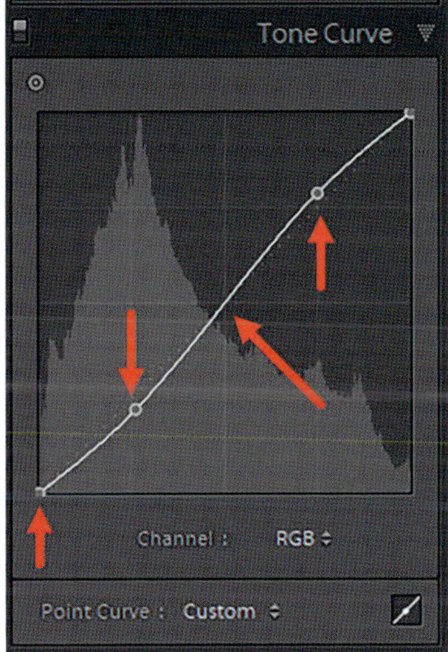

Figure 7.7a
The Tone Curve

Figure 7.7b
I like to incorporate two adjustable points for the highlights and shadows, and try to keep the midtones as close to the middle as possible. If the image is underexposed, I will try to raise it up.

point upward to fade out the black parts of the photo (figure 7.7b). This can give an "artsy" feel to the image and make the tones seem closer together, as seen in figure 7.8. You can do the opposite adjustments to make an image appear more "flat" by raising the shadows and dropping the highlights.

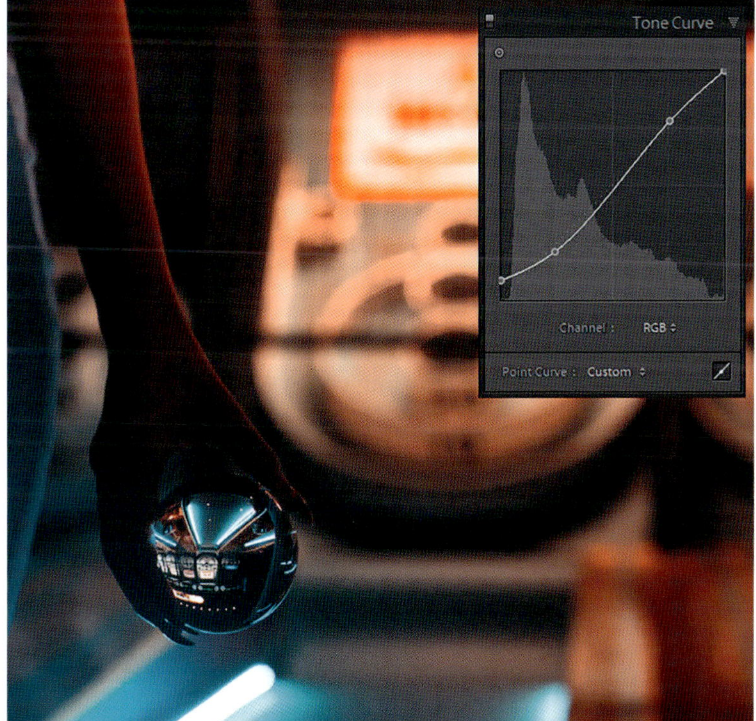

Figure 7.8
Raising the darkest point of the Tone Curve will lift the "blacks" of an image for a film-styled photo. I typically use this if my image is too dark and I want to bring up the tones.

The Tone Curve panel also works to add or subtract individual colors for color correction or color grading. I don't use this too often, but the gist is that moving the points higher or lower will add the color or add its complement, respectively (figure 7.9). Depending on which points you adjust, you can add those colors in the shadows or highlights, which can produce a split-tone look. Similarly, this can also be done in the Split Toning module, but this is a more controlled approach.

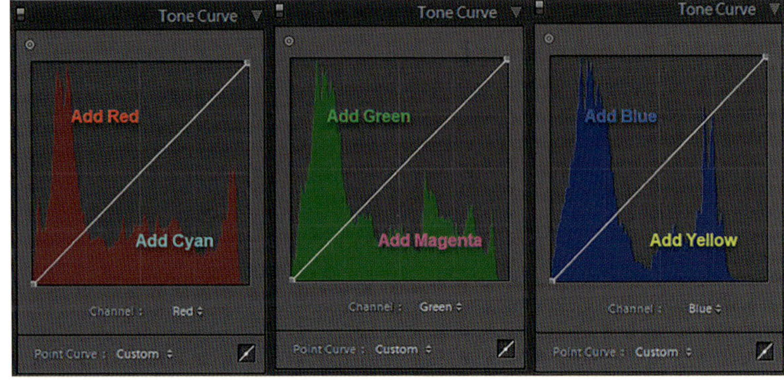

Figure 7.9

The Tone Curve can also be used to adjust what colors you want present in the highlights, midtones, and shadows of an image.

Calibration Panel

Next I move to the Calibration panel (figure 7.10). This is by far my most-used panel, as it can drastically improve the overall look of your photo. This may not work with every photo, but I use this 90 percent of the time. Most beginner photo editors leave this feature untouched since it is not very clear what it does and the settings are not that straightforward.

The Calibration panel is split up into the Shadows and the three Red, Green, and Blue Primaries. Typically, each camera's make and model has its own calibrated color profile. For example, Canon's color science has been more preferable than Sony's when it comes to shooting portraits. Canon features better color capture for skin tones, with an emphasis on warm orange tones. Sony seems to capture more greens and images may need additional color grading. This does not mean one camera brand is better than the other, but as an owner of both Canon and Sony cameras, I do prefer the color output of Canon. Because of the differences among cameras, editing softwares have camera calibration settings to make minor adjustments and correct certain colors from the raw file.

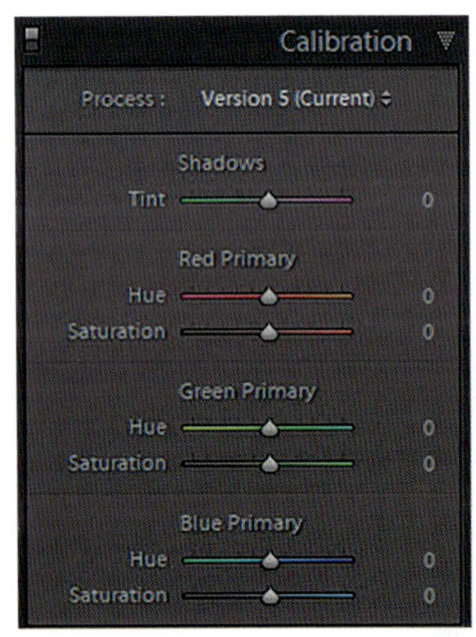

Figure 7.10

The Calibration panel in Lightroom

So, why does this matter? Understanding the reason something exists is the first step to knowing how to use it. The bulk of the Calibration tool allows you to alter the overall color mixture of your image. This is different from moving the sliders around in the HSL panel because this will affect every single pixel in the image that contains those colors rather than target the pixels with the specific hues. All the pixels in an image are made up of red, green, and blue values. Looking at the highlights/whites of an image (figure 7.11a and 7.11b) will show a higher percentage of all the color values, whereas examining the shadows/blacks of an image (figure 7.11a and 7.11c) will show a lower percentage. This is because white is composed of all colors, whereas black is the lack of any color.

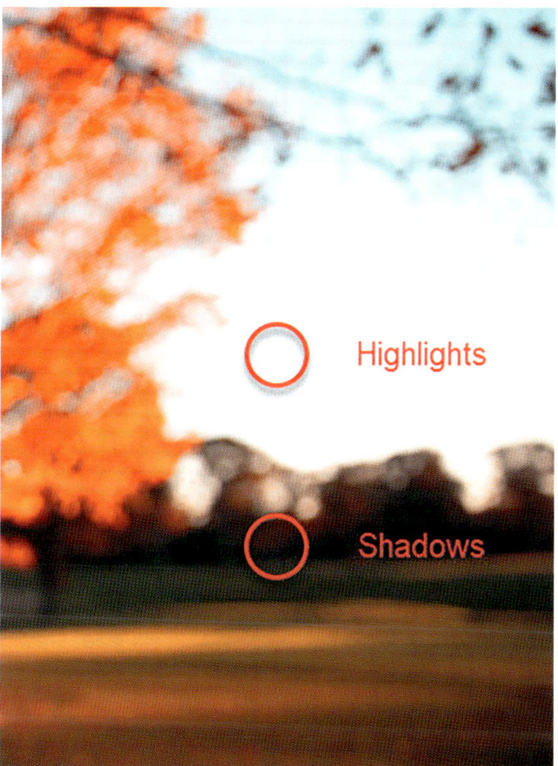

Figure 7.11a
This showcases where in the image I sampled from for the histograms shown in figures 7.13b and 7.13c.

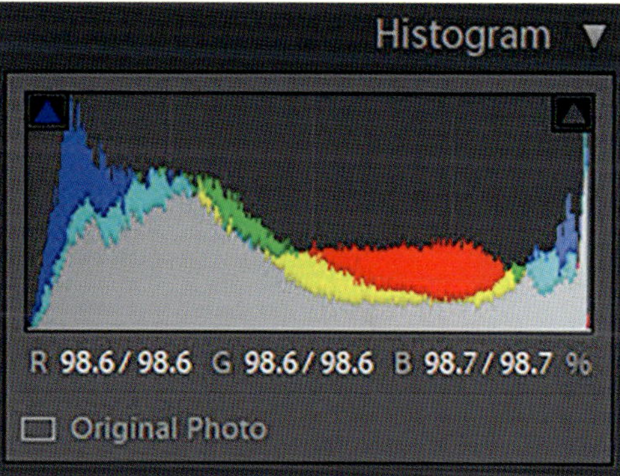

Figure 7.11b
The color values under the histogram chart illustrate a higher value of all colors in the white parts of an image.

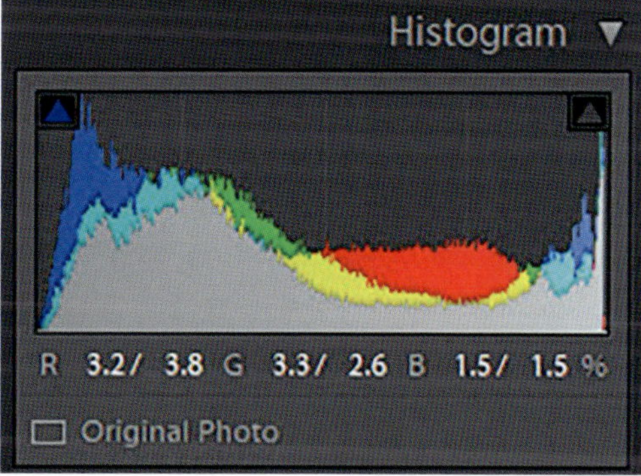

Figure 7.11c
The color values under the histogram chart illustrate a lower value of all colors in the black parts of an image.

This is also true when sampling the primary colors of an image. The pixels that make up red, for example, are not all red pixels. They consist of a ratio of reds, blues, and greens that make up specific colors (figure 7.12). Knowing this, you can understand why desaturating the Red Primary slider will desaturate all the colors present in the image (figure 7.13). This works the same way when adjusting the Hue sliders. This is why adjusting the color sliders in the Calibration panel will modify the look of the overall photo. The Shadows Tint slider is fairly easy to use and it modifies the green and magenta colors that lie in the shadows.

When it comes to color grading my images, I typically use the Calibration panel to set the final tone of the image. With a simple adjustment, you can make your images pop (figure 7.14a). From my experience, I've found that setting the Hue ratios to Red 2: Green 1: Blue -4, the image appears pleasing to the eye and develops what's called a Teal-Orange color grade. Increasing the values to a 50:25:-100 ratio will provide you with a lot of color contrast (figure 7.14b). You can drop it down to a 25:15:-50 for a more subtle pop (figure 7.14c). This is not a set rule and it may not work for every image, but it is a great starting point to understand how the values work and how they can liven up the image. Play around with the sliders and you may even find something new you like.

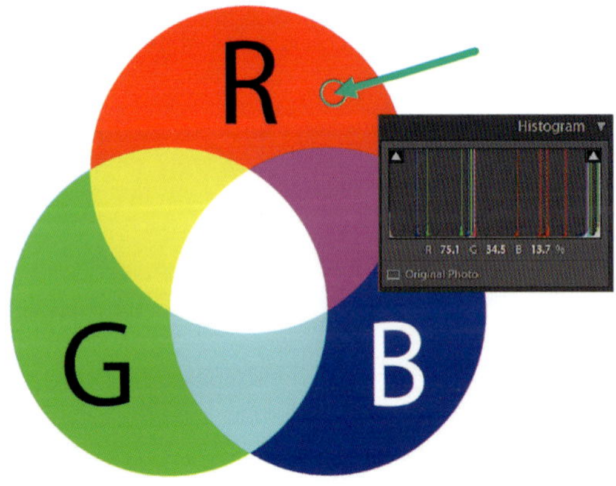

Figure 7.12
The red in an image contains a mixture of 75.1% Red, 34.5% Green, and 13.7% Blue Pixels.

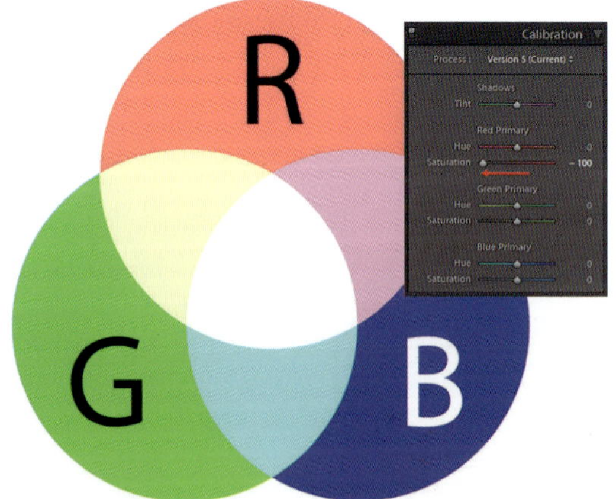

Figure 7.13
Dragging the Red Primary Saturation slider desaturates not only the red in the image, but every other color as well.

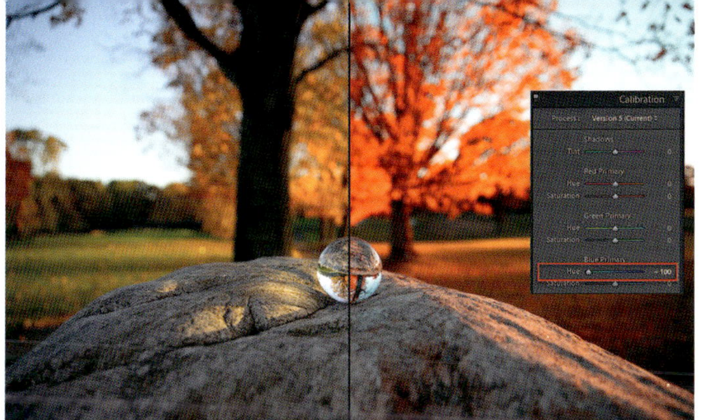

Figure 7.14a
Just moving the Blue Primary Hue toward Cyan can give the photo an "infrared" look.

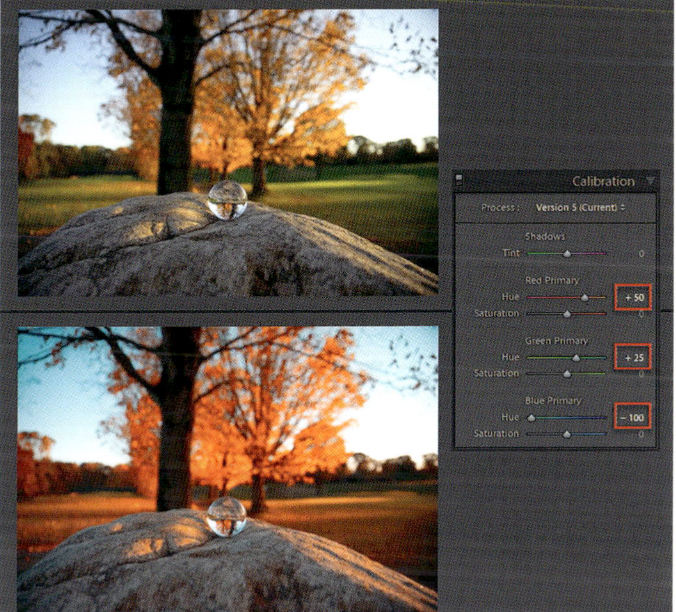

Figure 7.14b
Further adjustments can be made to mold the color contrast for a Teal-Orange color grade. After playing around with this panel, I noticed that the ratio in the figure gives me the best results. You can play around with the values to see what you like.

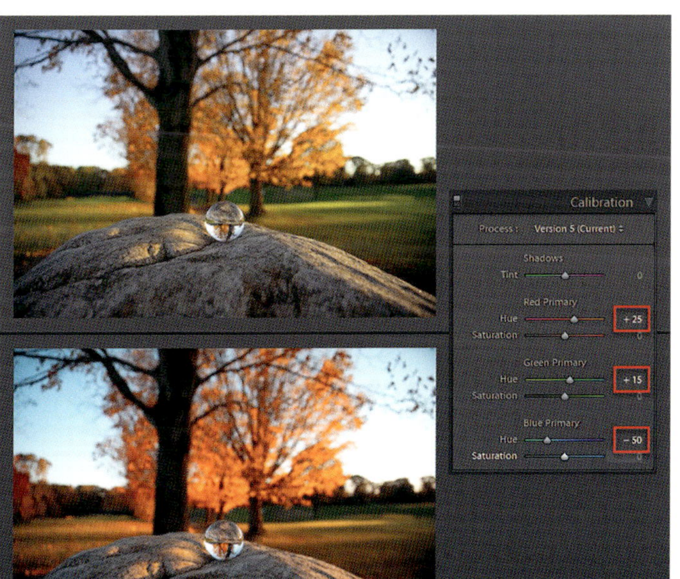

Figure 7.14c
An example of how reducing the ratio will maintain the complementary color contrast while still making your photo stand out. I generally find this works best for images that have reflective light.

HSL/Color Panel

Once you have an idea of the color scheme you want for your photo, move on to the HSL/Color panel to manually adjust the Hue, Saturation, and Luminance of each color. Similar to the Calibration panel, the HSL/Color panel looks equally convoluted but is pretty easy to understand once you practice with it. This panel allows you to either view each of the components separately or view all of them at the same time (figure 7.15a). During my editing process, I like to keep all of them visible so I can see how each setting is affecting

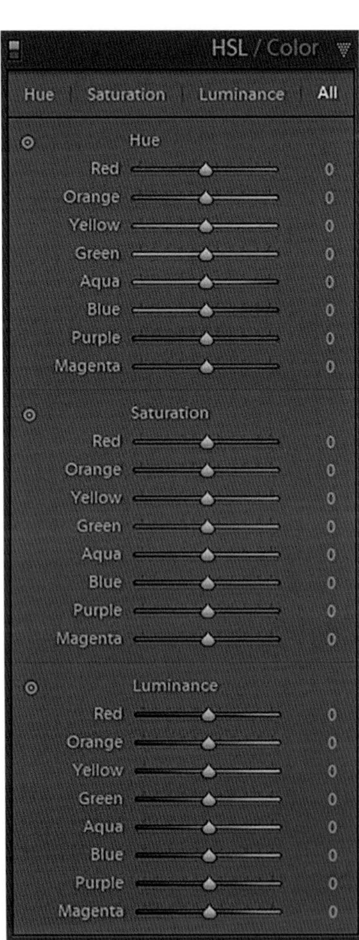

Figure 7.15a (left)
The HSL/Color panel allows you to adjust the Hue, Saturation, and Luminance of each color separately.

Figure 7.15b (right)
The Color tab functions exactly the same as the HSL tab, but the sliders are grouped by color.

the look of my photo. The Color tab basically presents the same settings, but they are grouped together by color instead of function (figure 7.15b). Either tab can be used depending on your workflow.

Following is a quick explanation of how each setting works. Hue is described as the tone of a color. For example, dragging the Hue slider for the color Red can change the existing reds in the image from magenta to orange when going from left to right. This slider has the most significant role when you're playing around with how colors stand out.

Saturation, as many of you know, controls whether you take out color or intensify the color. One thing to be careful to avoid is oversaturating one color in your image without modifying the adjacent colors. This can lead to unwanted color clipping (figure 7.16).

Figure 7.16
Adjusting the Saturation too far to the right can create unwanted elements.

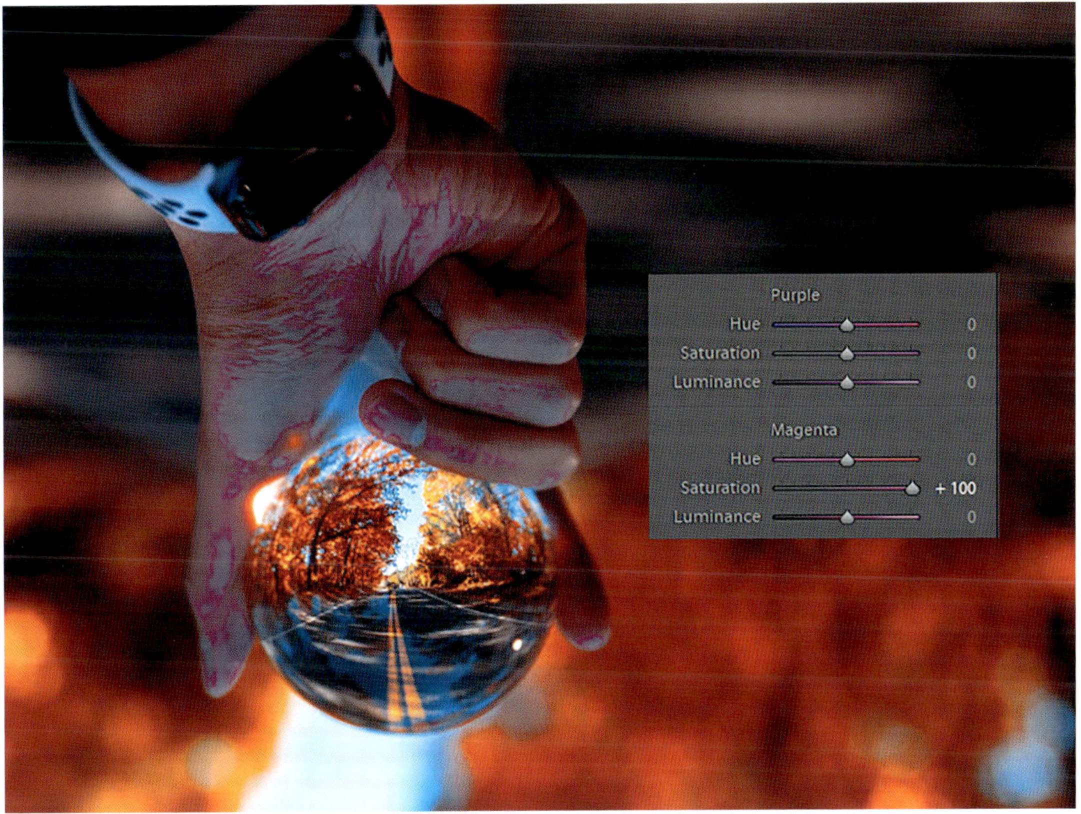

The last option, Luminance, can be used to brighten or darken a specific color. I typically do this in the later part of my color grading so I can fine-tune the mood of the image. Most of the time, I only make small adjustments to one or two colors if I want them to be more or less apparent in the image (figure 7.17).

When using the HSL/Color panel, I first go through each color and play around with the Hue sliders to see what needs to be modified. Next, I adjust the Saturation of any color that I feel needs to be strengthened. If I notice a certain color is oversaturated, I will increase the Luminosity to weaken its presence. My biggest advice with color manipulation is to keep practicing and eventually you will find your own style. If needed, you can try out some Lightroom presets and learn how those work with certain images. Once you master your understanding of these settings, you will be able to make your own to speed up your color-grading workflow.

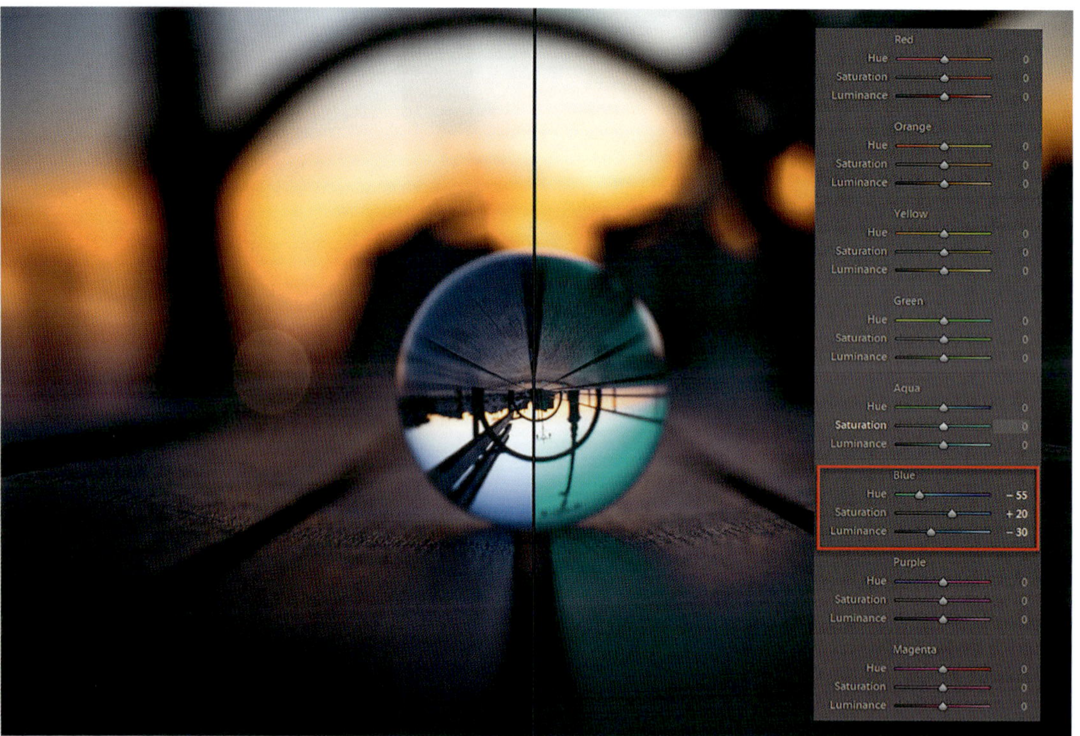

Figure 7.17

An example of how adjusting the settings for one color does not affect the rest of the image, unlike adjustments made in the Calibration panel. Sliding the Hue toward the left for Blue will result in a turquoise-teal appearance.

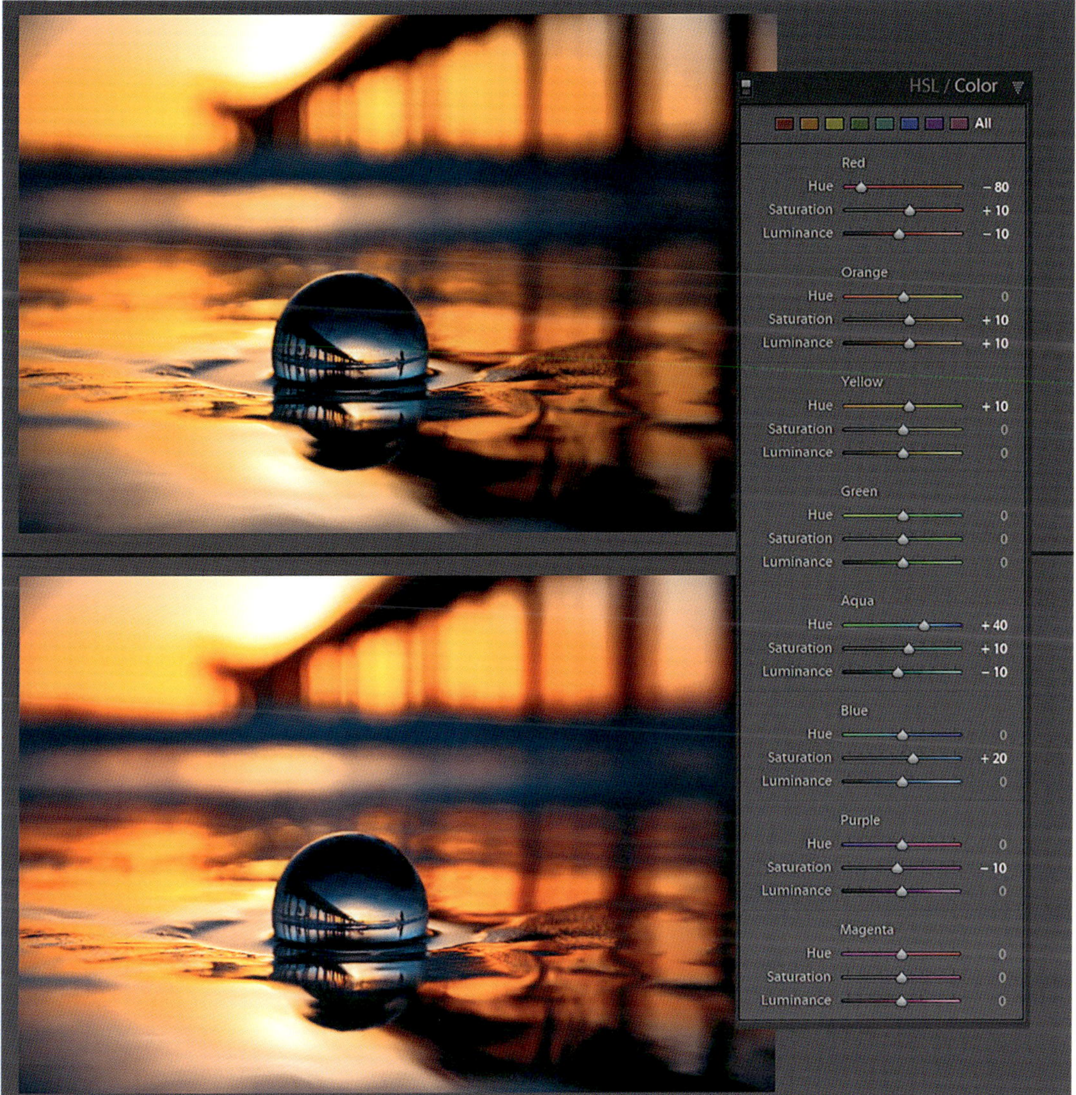

Figure 7.18
The HSL sliders should be used to make subtle adjustments to boost or dilute specific colors in the image.

Graduated and Radial Filters

Some other tools to mention are the Graduated filter and Radial filter. I consider these secondary tools that I use to add a more dramatic look to my lensball photos. When making changes in the Basic panel, everything in the image is modified. If you want a more specific

The Graduated and Radial filters can be found up here. When clicking either of them, you will be presented with a group of settings similar to those in the Basic panel. These settings are applied only to the areas of the image where you place the filters.

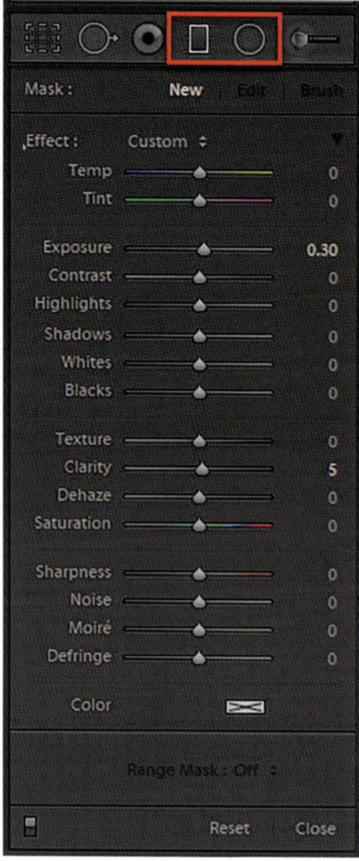

approach to these changes, these two filters will allow for that. When you select either tool, you will see most of the settings from the Basic panel, but these will only affect the parts of the image to which you apply the filter (figure 7.19).

As the name implies, the Graduated filter will apply the changes gradually as you drag it onto the image. As seen in figure 7.20, dragging the filter downward from the top of the image will apply the settings from 100% opacity to 0%, as highlighted in red. The two lines on the top and bottom of the midline dictate how smooth or abrupt the transition will be. The closer they are, the harsher the change will appear. When using this setting, I usually will add negative exposure values and drag inward from the four corners for a vignette effect, or do the opposite to bring up detail with a positive exposure. You can equip these filters with higher saturation or temperature to mimic sun rays coming from a corner, or stack multiple filters for a balanced feel. If one side of your image is underexposed, you can apply multiple positive exposure filters from that side to even it out.

Next we have the Radial filter. This is probably the most applicable change you can make to dramatically improve the separation between the lensball and the backdrop. Similar to the Graduated filter, the settings for this filter are essentially the same as those found in the Basic panel. When using the Radial filter, I create the adjustment over the subject of my image, which in this case is the ball, and have the effects bleed out from the middle to the edge of the circle (figure 7.22). You can hold down the Ctrl key on your keyboard while dragging out this filter to create a perfect circle.

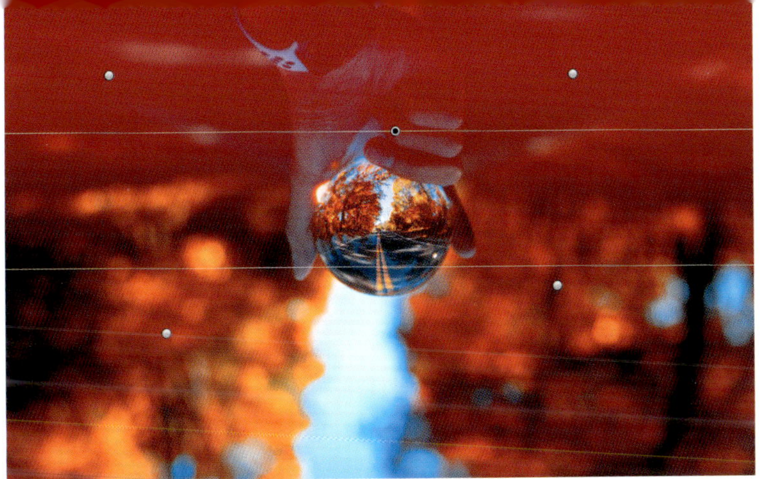

Figure 7.20
A visual illustration of how the Graduated filter is applied to a photo. The further apart the lines, the more gradual the transition, and the closer the lines, the tighter the transition.

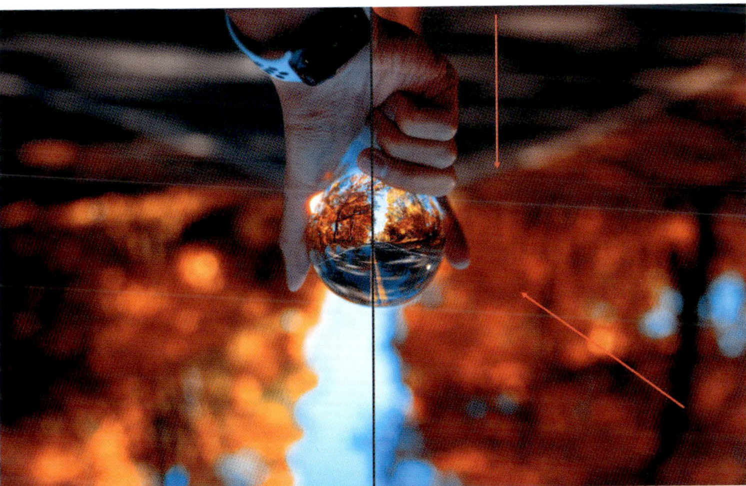

Figure 7.21
A before (left side) and after (right side) example of using a warm Graduated filter from the top and bottom corners. It might not be too noticeable, but I am able to increase the warm tones of my hand and the road without affecting the cool parts of the image.

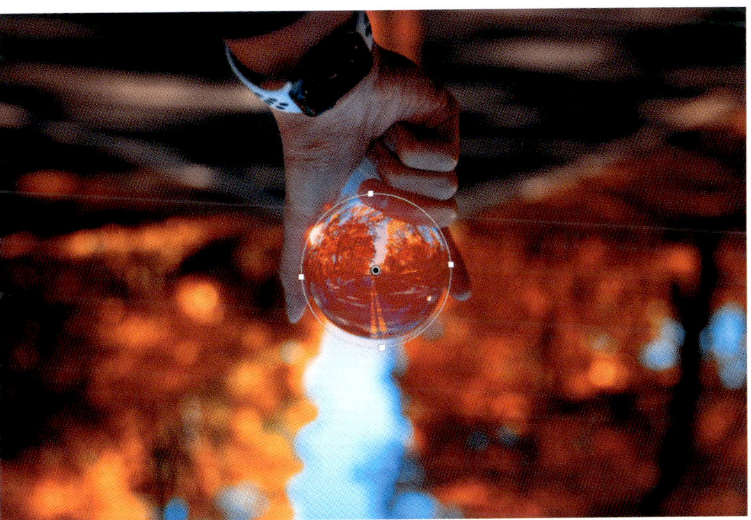

Figure 7.22
The Radial filter is a great tool to use for lensball photos to draw out more detail or create a higher contrast between the subject and the background.

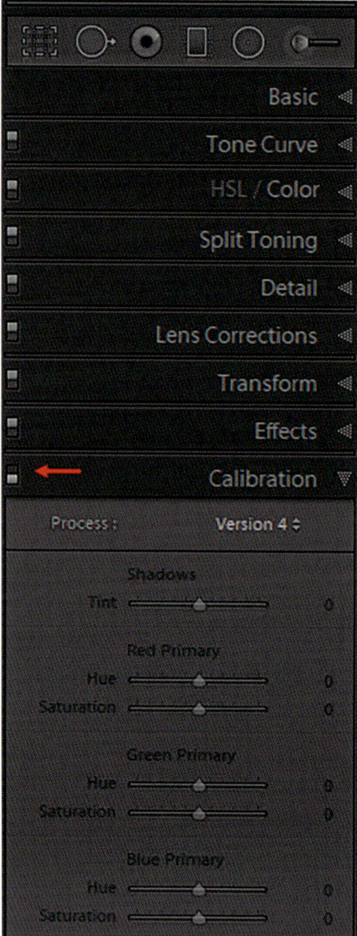

As for the adjustments, I like to increase the Exposure, Contrast, and Clarity inside the ball, as that should be the main focus of the lensball photo. Additional masks can be applied over the hand holding the ball, for example, since it is in the foreground with the ball. Be mindful of the Feathering setting, as too low of a value can create a hard edge in the filter, which may not look realistic. I tend to just leave my masks at 50% for a subtle feathering. This concept can be applied to any type of photo to draw attention to certain subjects.

Turn Your World Upside Down

One of the questions I am asked most frequently is how to flip the image of the lensball when editing. The simple answer is to use Photoshop. If you're working in Lightroom, you can easily bring the photo over to Photoshop by right-clicking (Mac: control + click) on the image and selecting "Edit in Adobe Photoshop…" from the context menu, or by pressing Ctrl + E (Mac: command + E) on your keyboard (figure 7.24). This will allow you to bring the photo back into Lightroom when you're done without have to reimport after your changes.

In terms of flipping the image, there are a few different methods to do this, but they are all relatively the same. The first step is done in camera. Make sure the ball's edge is as viewable as possible and is not obstructed by distractions such as your hand. If there is no way around this, you can try your best to mask it out when editing, but it

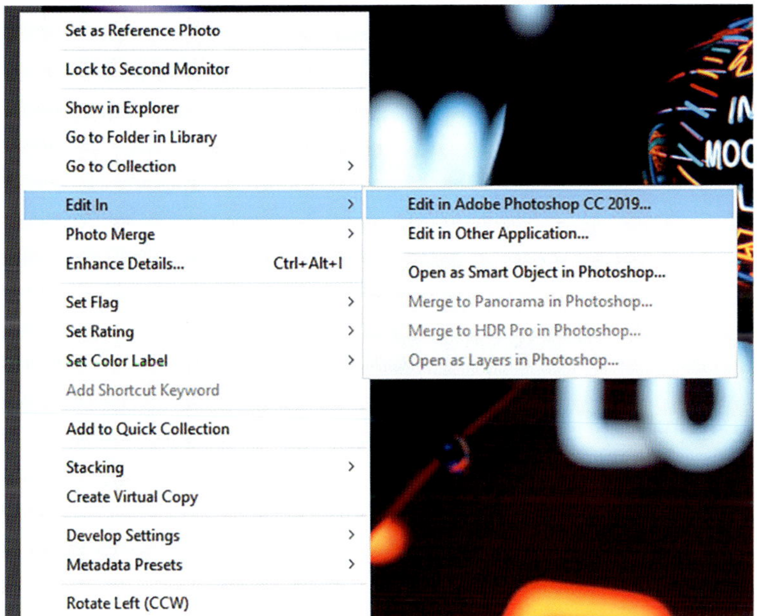

Figure 7.24

Lightroom makes it easy to move files back and forth with Photoshop so you do not have to reimport the files when you're done working on them. You can also bring photos back into Photoshop and make further layer adjustments later on.

will make your process longer. Another thing to note is that you want to shoot the ball level with your camera so that the perspective of the inside image does not stand out after you are done flipping it.

Once you have the image in Photoshop, create a new layer by pressing Ctrl + Shift + N (Mac: command + shift + N) or clicking the New Layer icon (figure 7.25a). Next, go up to the Marquee tool in the toolbar and choose the Elliptical Marquee tool (figure 7.25b) so that you can draw a circle over the lensball. Just as in Lightroom, you can hold down the Shift key and drag to create a perfect circle. I like to leave a slight gap between the marquee circle and the edge of the ball, making the marquee circle slightly smaller than the ball so I do not accidentally select the background around the ball when I flip. You also do not want to interfere with the edge of the glass ball because it is fairly difficult to replicate the warp effect in post-production.

Once you have the selection over the lensball (figure 7.25c), go to *Select > Modify > Feather,* or press Shift + F6, to bring up the Feather Selection tool (figure 7.25d). Feathering gives you a soft edge for

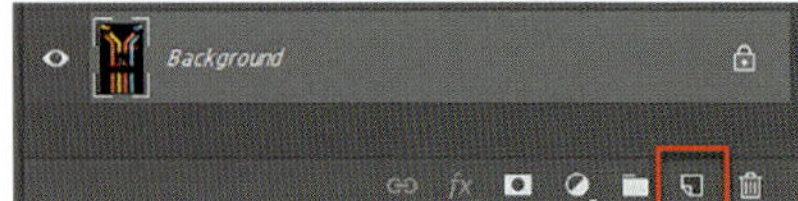

Figure 7.25a

Create a new layer by hitting this icon or pressing Ctrl + Shift + N (Mac: command + shift + N).

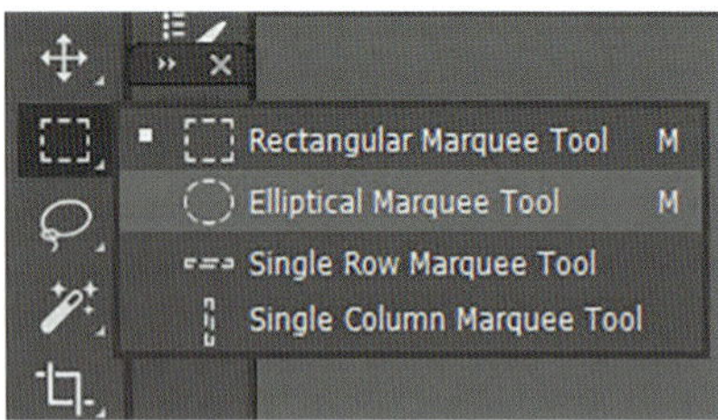

Figure 7.25b

The Elliptical Marquee tool can be found by right-clicking the Marquee icon at the top of the toolbar. Cycle through the Marquee tools by hitting the M key.

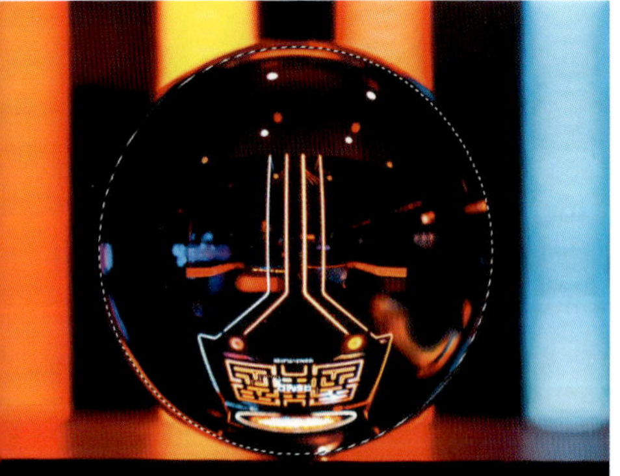

Figure 7.25c

You can either hold down Shift and drag to create a circle, or, my preferred method, hold Shift + Alt (Mac: shift + option) while dragging from the center out so.

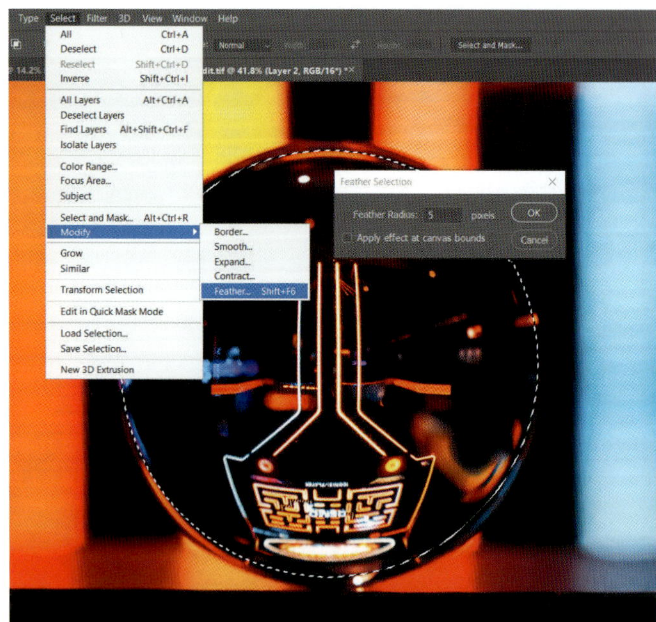

Figure 7.25d

The Feather Selection tool can be used to soften the edge of your selection so that you are not met with a noticeable hard edge in the final picture. I set this value at either 5 or 10, depending on what aperture I used and the distance between the lensball and camera.

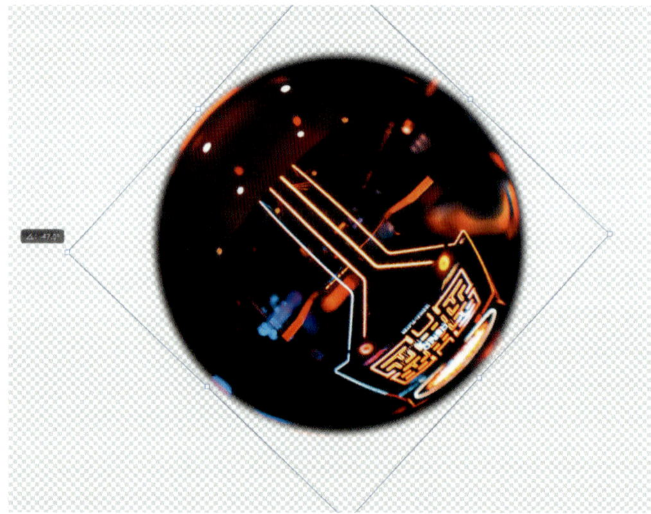

Figure 7.25e

Now you should have an adjustable copy of the lensball that you can freely rotate or flip by using the Free Transform function (PC: Ctrl + T; Mac: command + T).

copying the lensball. Increasing the value will allow the edge to be softer, but the original image will start bleeding into the selection. I like to set this around 5 to 10, depending on how I captured the original photo.

Once this is done, select the original Background layer and copy and paste it as a new layer. Now you can freely rotate or vertical flip the selection with the Free Transform tool (PC: Ctrl + T; Mac: command + T) (figure 7.25e). If you captured other things you want to remove, you can mask them in the selection layer with brushes.

Once you've achieved the desired look, bring the image back over to Lightroom by hitting Ctrl + S (Mac: command + S). And there you have it, a quick five-step tutorial on how to rotate/flip a lensball image.

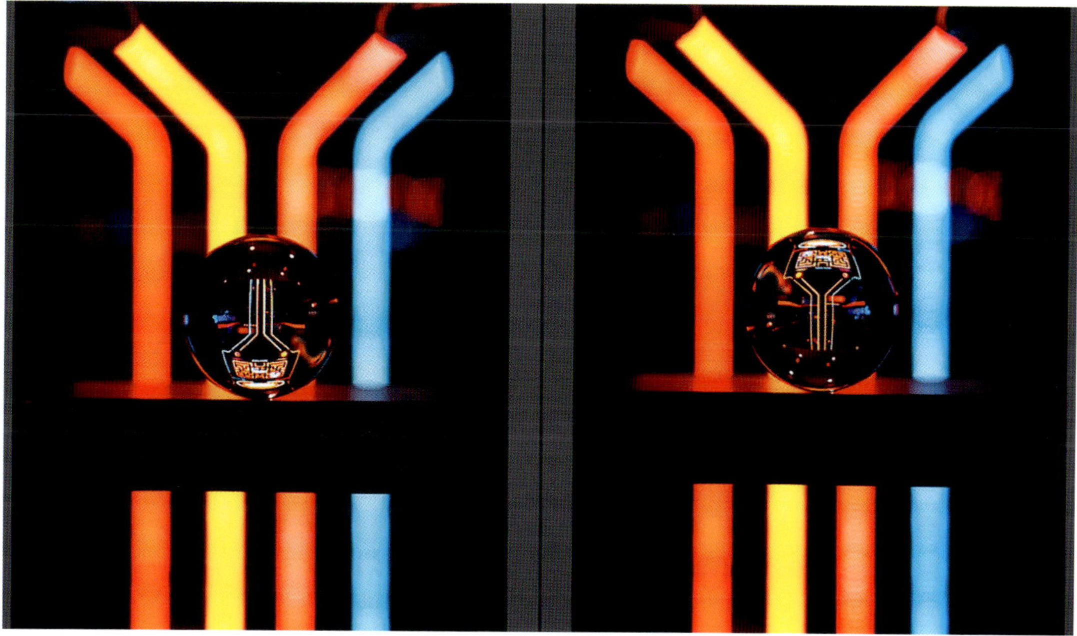

Figure 7.26a
A before and after of the vertical flip.

Figure 7.26b
Try to capture the initial image
with no obstructions at the
edge of the lensball for a
quick and painless flip.

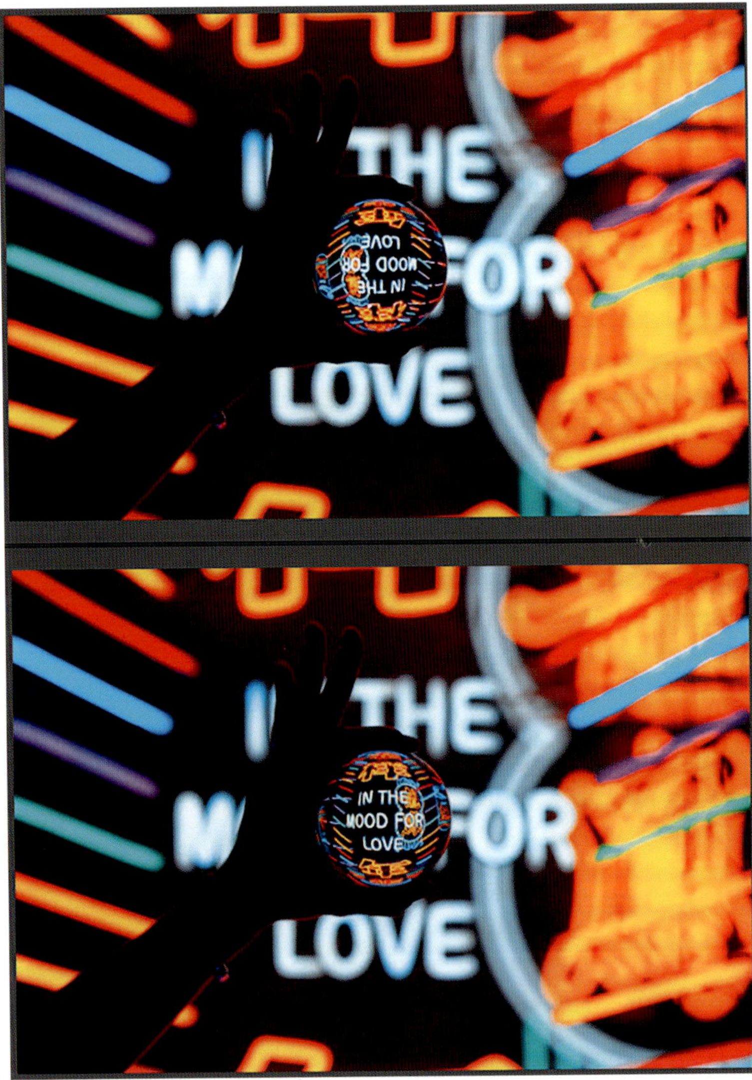

CHAPTER 8

You Do You

Although all the previous chapters appear to be set rules and guidelines on how to shoot, the last chapter is for encouraging you to develop your own style. There have been many times when I have been inspired by compositions and edits others have used for their photos and tried to incorporate them into my own work. Nowadays, every photographer knows the technical aspects of how to properly expose a scene and press the shutter button, but what is hard to come by are those who challenge themselves to test new techniques and concepts. Inspiration may not always lead to creation, but it is the culmination of ideas you gather through viewing someone's portfolio that spark ideas for your own work. In this chapter, I will provide some examples that I tried out for fun just because it is nice to entertain certain concepts.

Self-Portraits

While it is difficult for people who like to be behind the camera to take self-portraits, it is something you ought to try out when you get the chance. I don't believe practice always makes perfect, but it does push you further toward the finish line than those who do not try. For my twenty-fifth birthday, I decided to try a self-portrait inside a lensball to see how it would turn out. As seen in figure 8.1a, the concept was to have me holding a lensball with me floating inside. This project consisted of three separate images to build what you see in the final image. Although it is not one of my best images, it was still extremely fun to do and can teach you different ways of photographing and post-processing. Figures 8.1b, 8.1c, and 8.1d break down the steps I took to create the final image.

This next shot is one of my most seen images, which was shot basically on a whim (figure 8.2a). The picture, titled *Reminiscence*, is composed of two separate photos taken on two different occasions that were warped together in Photoshop. Figure 8.2b is the first picture I ever took of a lensball, which wasn't even mine. My friend Michael decided to bring the ball to the beach as a prop during one of our

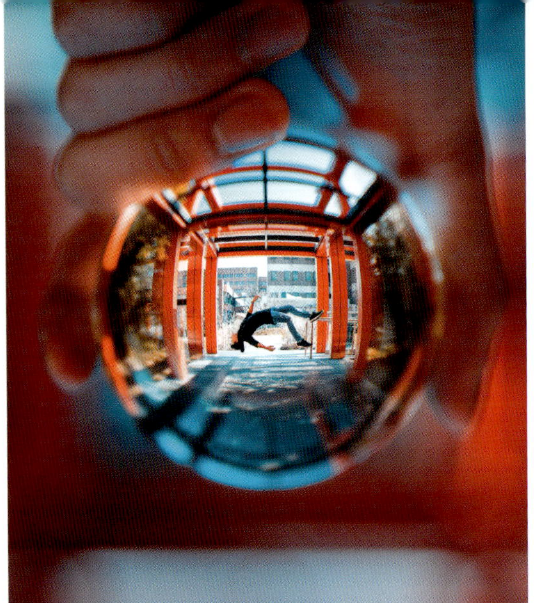

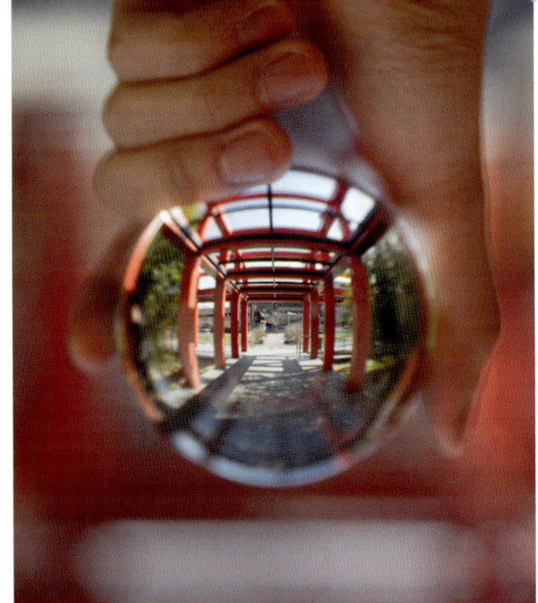

Figure 8.1a

70mm | F/2.8 | 1/640s | ISO 100

This photo was captured at the entrance of one of my university buildings and is a composite of three separate images.

Figure 8.1b

70mm | F/2.8 | 1/640s | ISO 100

This is the first shot to develop the overall setting and how I wanted the frame to look. Things I look for are overall leading lines or interesting colors.

Figure 8.1c

50mm | F/2.8 | 1/250s | ISO 100

The next step was to capture myself (with a remote shutter) to later place in the ball. I had the camera placed on a tripod at a similar height as where I took the original photo. Looking back, I should have used a wider lens to capture more of the environment so I could warp it better with the original image.

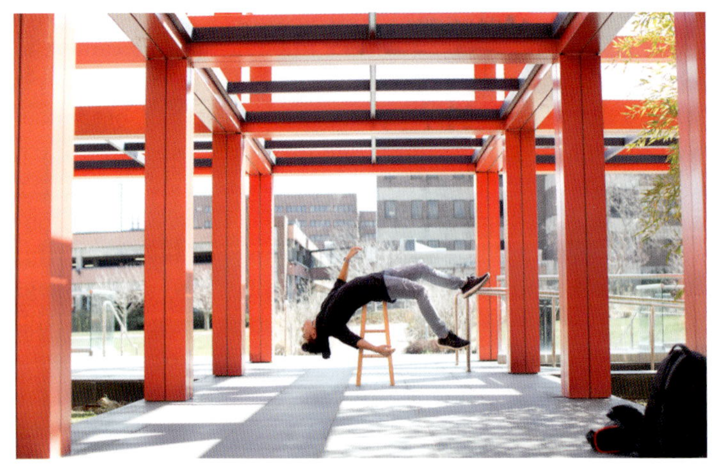

Figure 8.1d

50mm | F/2.8 | 1/250s | ISO 100

This was shot seconds after the self-portrait so I could use the background to remove the stool I was resting on. Having multiple captures of a background can facilitate any removal editing you may want to do when you get home.

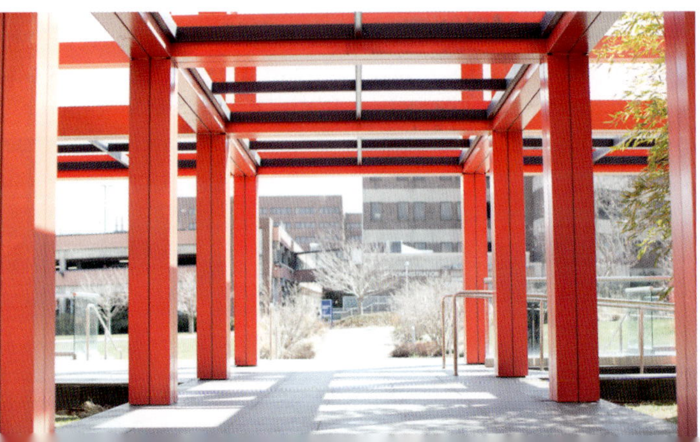

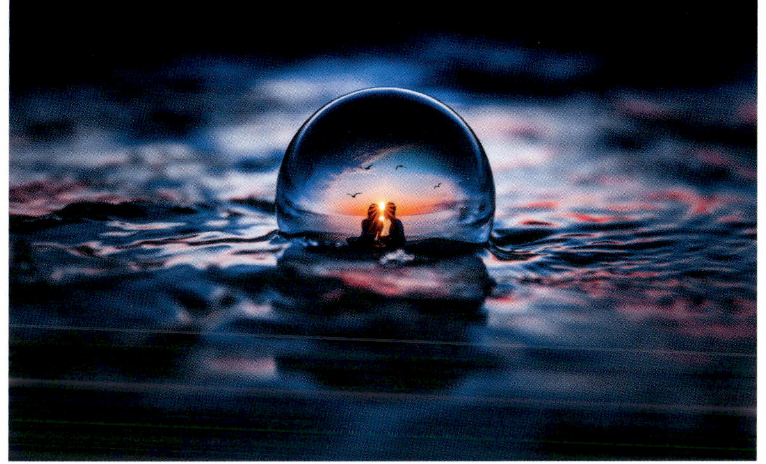

Figure 8.2a

70mm | F/2.8 | 1/125s | ISO 100

This image consists of two separate photos (figures 8.2b and 8.2c) that were color graded to match the overall tone. The self-portrait was masked out into a circle, which was then warped into a curved image to match the inside of the lensball.

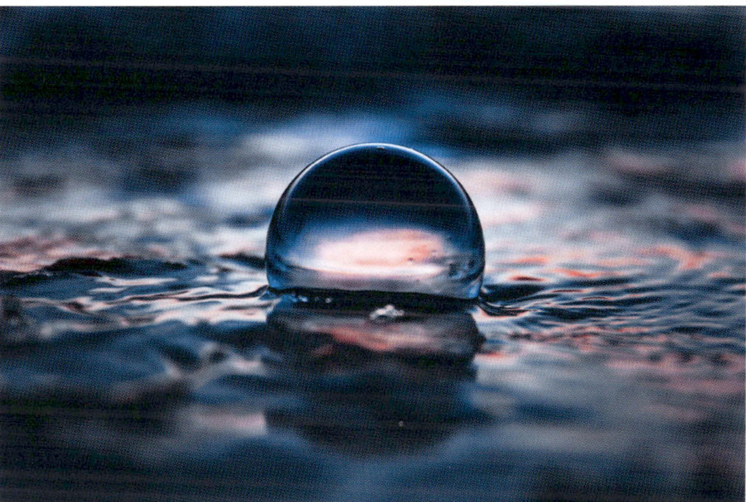

Figure 8.2b

70mm | F/2.8 | 1/125s | ISO 100

This is my first lensball image ever. Nothing too exciting and there was a complete void in the middle of the ball. I kept it in my Lightroom library in case I had a use for it one day.

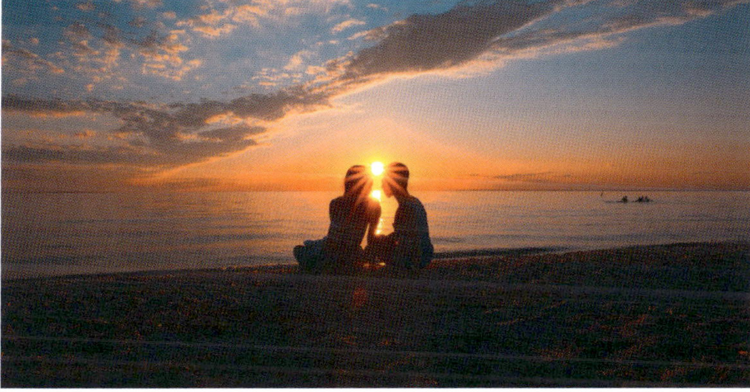

Figure 8.2c

24mm | F/2.8 | 1/250s | ISO 100

The camera was set up on a mini tripod and captured the photo with a timer. At the time, I did not own an infrared remote, so there were many shots of me running back and forth to readjust and capture. This was the couple self-portrait I took of Nicole and I at our favorite beach when we first started dating. Side note, this is the same location where I proposed to her.

shoots. I took a few shots of it on the sand and in the water and didn't think much of it for a while. I didn't even create the final image until a few months later when I thought of a neat idea for a couple portrait for Nicole and I.

Figure 8.2c was an initial couple self-portrait I took with Nicole earlier that summer, and I saw that I could color grade it to match the tones in the lensball photo. After a few back-and-forth edits, I created one of the most recognized lensball photos just because I had an idea and ran with it. You never know when you will create your masterpiece unless you go out and keep capturing.

Create Props for Your Prop

There are some photos where your props may need props (figure 8.3a). At one point in my photography career, I designed bokeh filters with intricate cut-out shapes that could be placed over your lens to transform the background lights into whatever the shape was (figure 8.3b). Figure 8.4 is an example of a snowflake filter I made to frame a lensball photo of a Christmas tree. My other hobbies like 3D printing integrated well into my lensball photography as I designed and printed different stands to hold up the ball for a Halloween themed shot (figure 8.5). Utilizing your other creative outlets can make your photos stand out from the rest.

Figure 8.3a

85mm | F/1.2 | 1/40s | ISO 100

I used a leaf bokeh filter in this image paired with some string lights in the back to resemble a spill of autumn from the cup. This was captured at my local Starbucks.

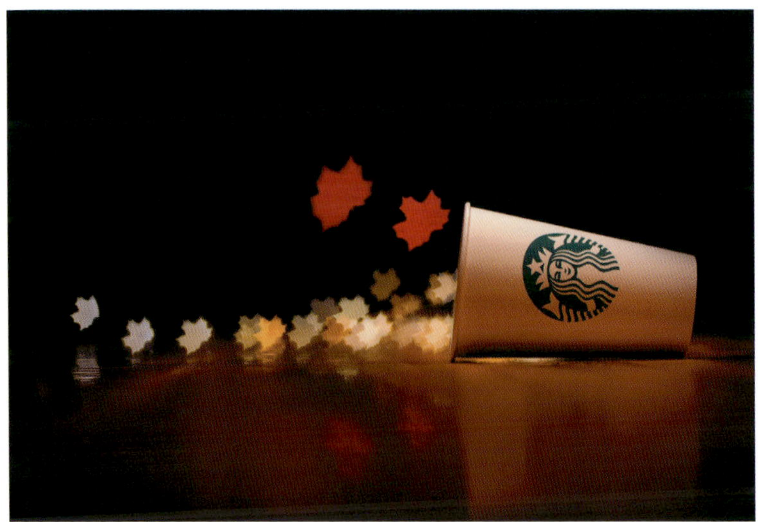

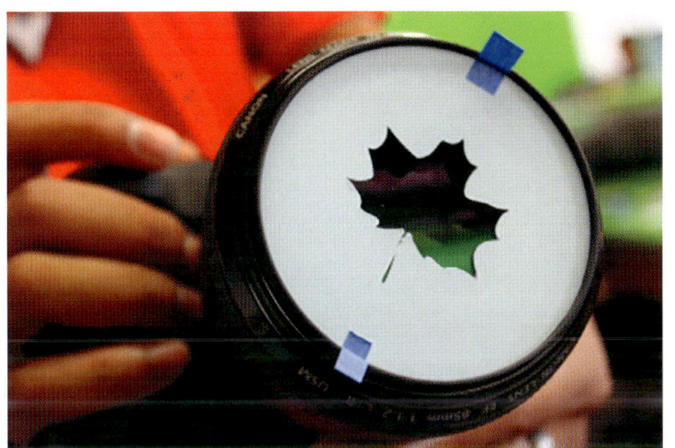

Figure 8.3b

These filters can either be created with a 3D printer or cut out on cardstock. The shape and size of the hole is contingent on the focal length and minimum aperture of the lens. It is better to shoot wide open with a prime lens than to be limited by a small aperture on a zoom lens.

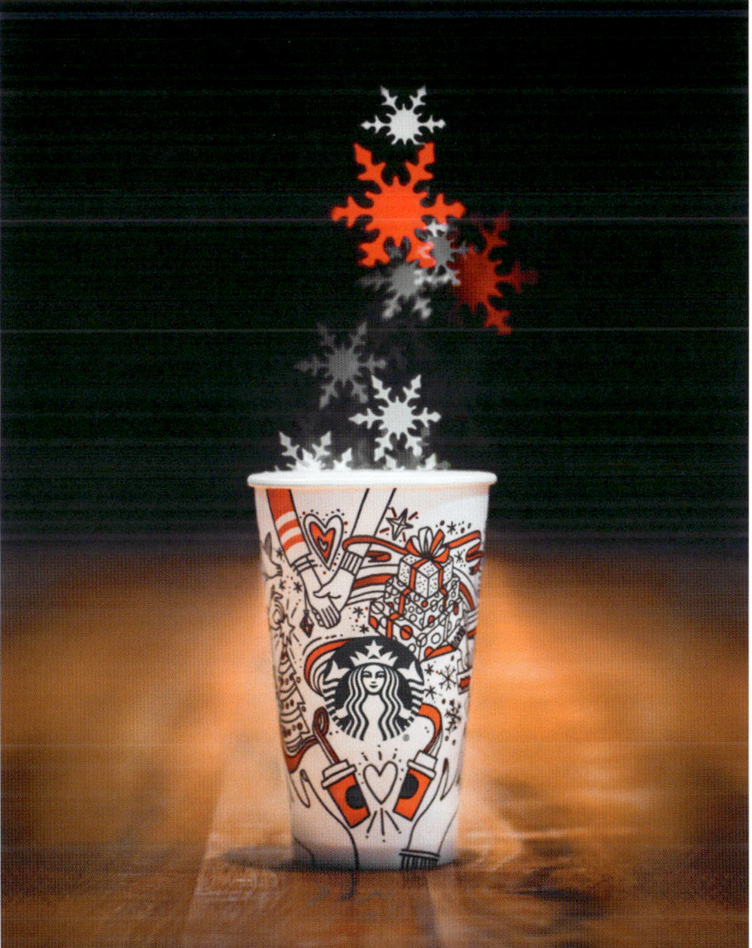

Figure 8.3c

85mm | F/1.2 | 1/60s | ISO 200

Shooting with a wide-open aperture like f/1.2 along with a telephoto lens will allow the bokeh lights in the background to appear bigger. The string lights were hung at the end of the long table in Starbucks, and the red snowflake is actually a traffic light outside the cafe.

Figure 8.4

85mm | F/1.4 | 1/100s | ISO 1600
This image was captured with my snowflake bokeh filter, which transformed the Christmas lights in the tree into the shape of snowflakes. Because this was shot on a telephoto lens like the 85mm, the background is extremely compressed and only show-cases the tree lights and not the empty space around the tree.

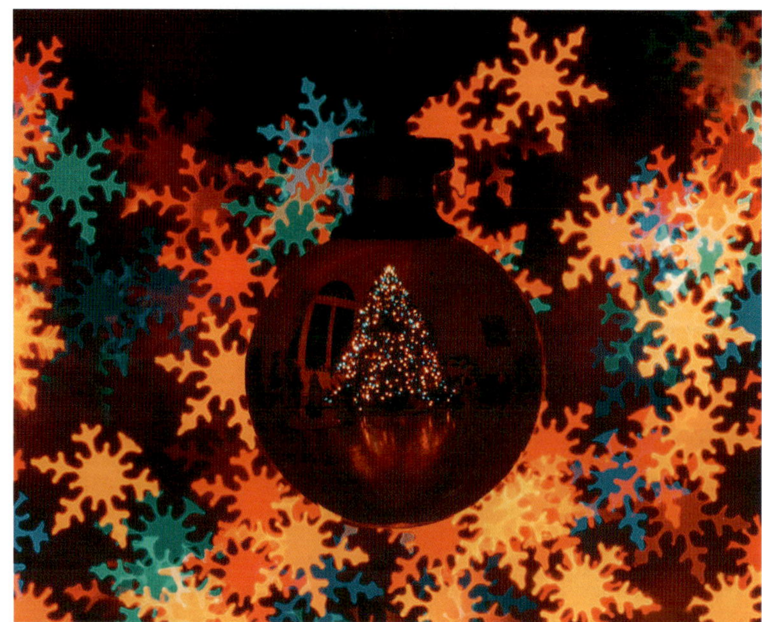

Figure 8.5

85mm | F/1.4 | 1/250s | ISO 250
I 3D printed a stand to hold up a lensball for a jack-o-lantern–style lensball image. The shape in the back was cut out and placed in front of a lamp, while I used string lights as leading lines toward the center of the image.

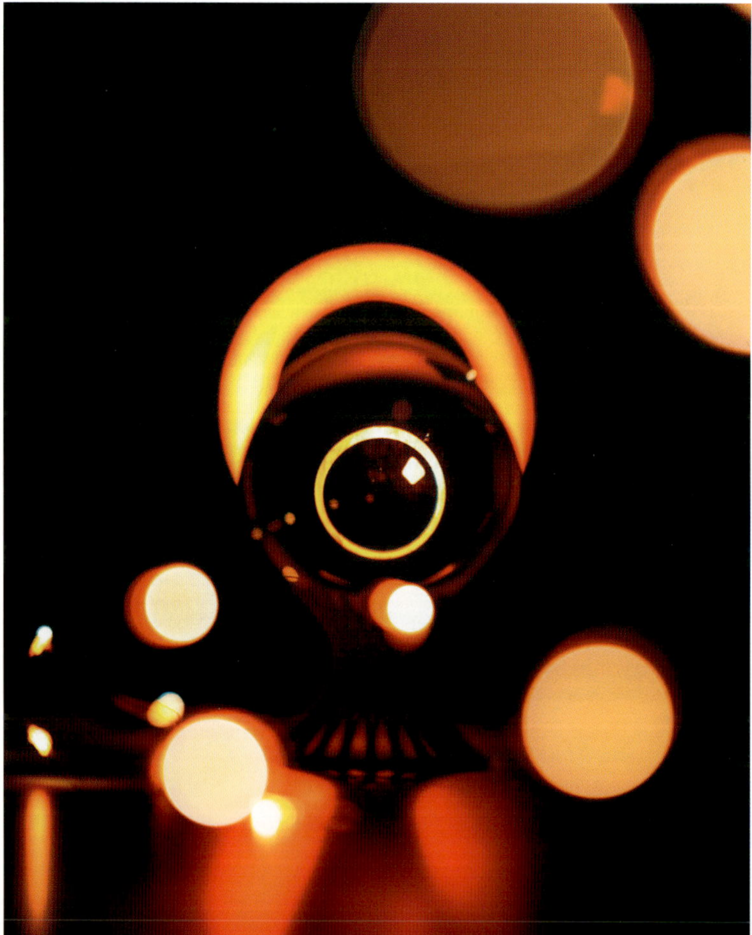

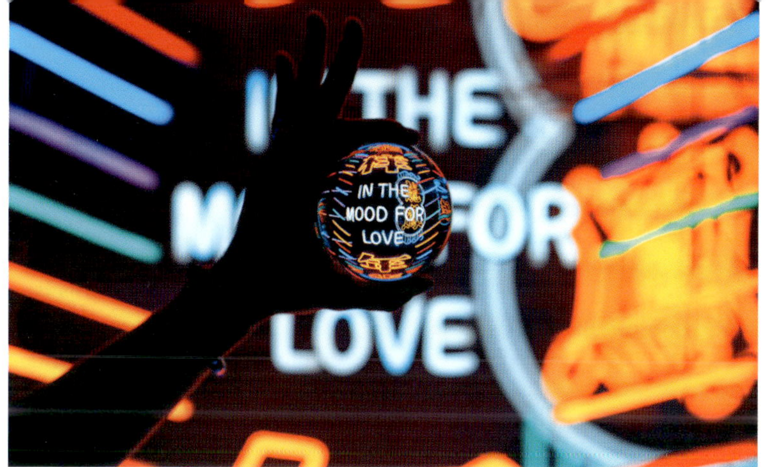

Figure 8.6
85mm | F/2.8 | 1/200s | ISO 100
Use the lensball to draw attention to text or phrases. If they have their own light source that is even better.

Figure 8.7b
50mm | F/2.8 | 1/100s | ISO 100
This can be a stretch, but try using the lensball to finish a phrase or sentence by having the initial text trail off into the background and then continue inversely within the ball. Again, these are just ideas to try out if you are looking for inspiration.

Word Play

Since the lensball is essentially a spherical magnifying glass, why not use it to highlight words or phrases for your photo? Placing the ball in front of neon text can help add emphasis to the message (figure 8.6). Typically, artsy neon signs have something meaningful to say, unless it is a sign for fast food. But because art is subjective, feel free to test it out and see which signs work best for your image.

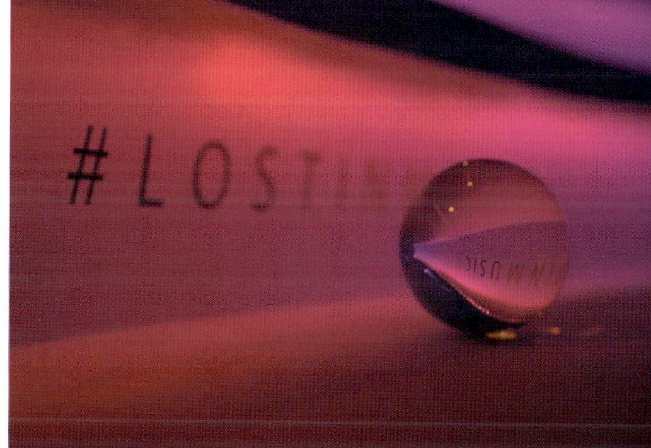

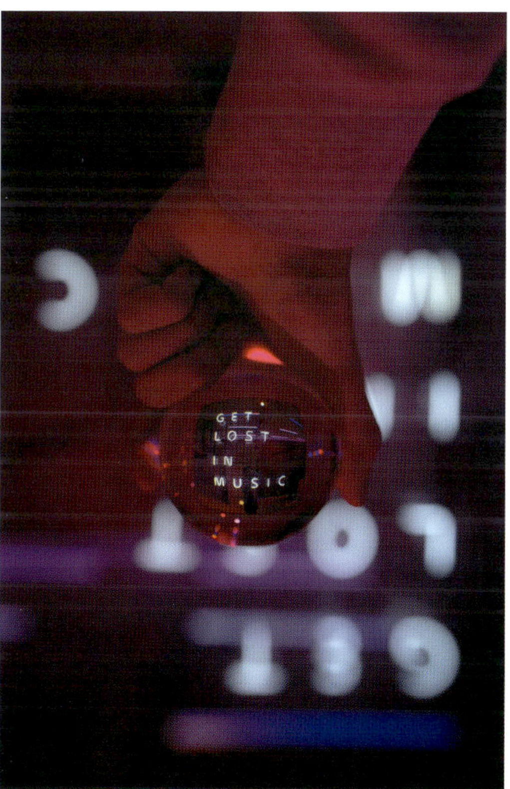

Figure 8.7a
50mm | F/2.8 | 1/100s | ISO 400
Another example of how text can be the subject of a lensball photo, as it forces it to the foreground and makes it the primary thing that is in focus.

Artificial Framing

Lastly, you can also resort to Photoshop when it comes to creating something interesting. To add an additional compositional element into your image, custom framing can be used to bring the viewer's attention into the image. For example, figure 8.8 features an inverse square frame of the image to outline the lensball. Although this isn't necessary for the photo, it does keep your attention a few seconds longer than if it wasn't there. I did this by stacking a double horizontal- and vertical-flipped image of the original photo as a layer in Photoshop, and then masking out a shape to act as a frame.

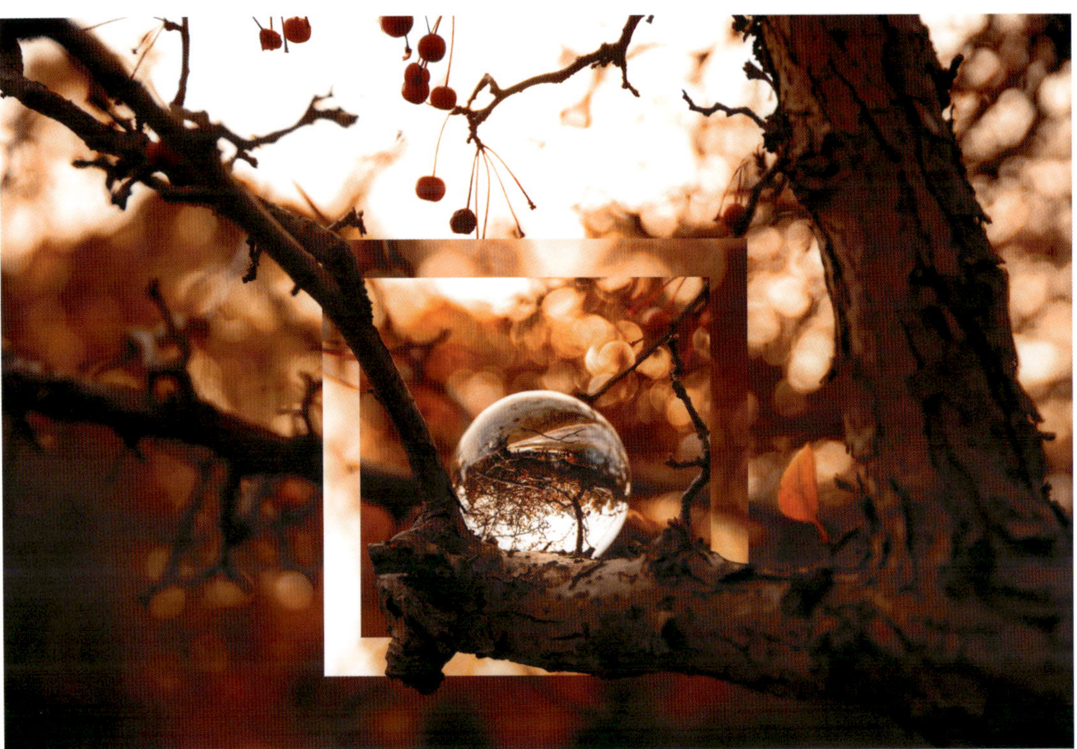

Figure 8.8
50mm | F/2.8 | 1/800s | ISO 100
This edit was created to "frame" an image within an image.

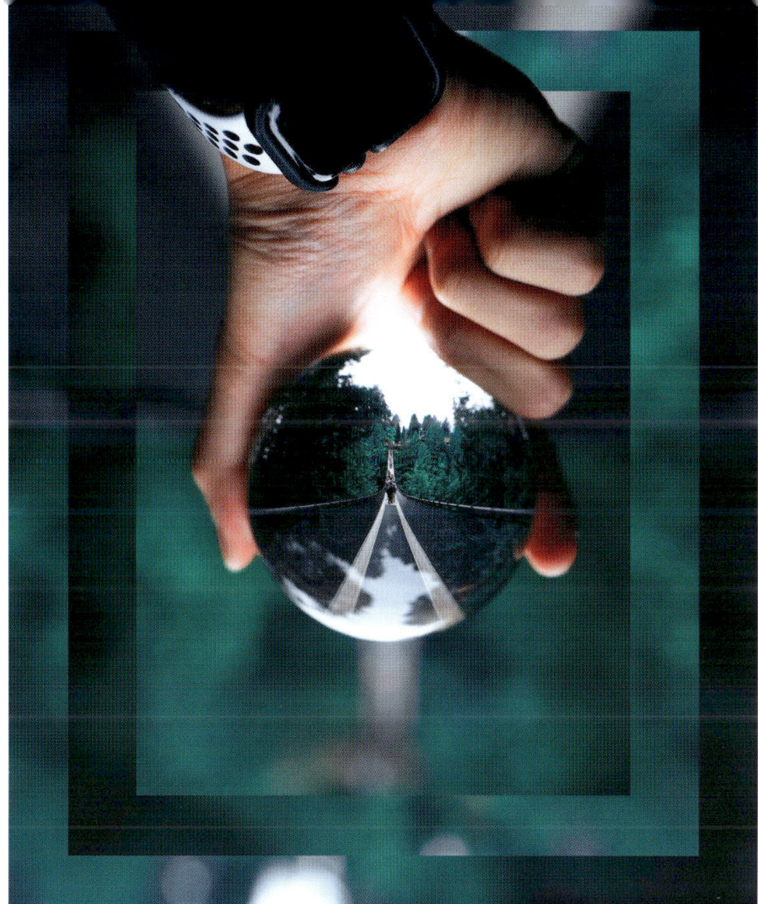

Figure 8.9
35mm | F/2.8 | 1/200s | ISO 100
Another example of using a rectangular frame in the image to match the 4:5 aspect ratio.

Figure 8.10
24mm | F/2.8 | 1/125s | ISO 250
Frames don't have to be constrained to a four-sided shape. Here, I created a custom hexagonal frame to stick with the theme of the hexagonal pattern in the backdrop.

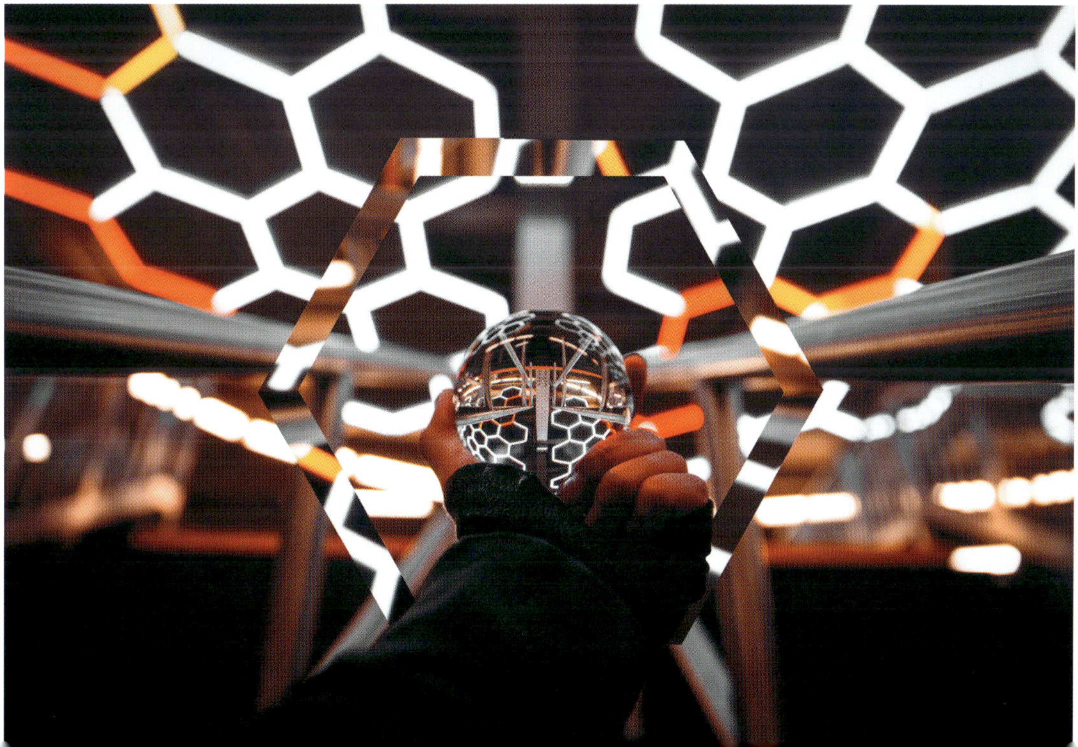

There are so many different ways to incorporate new ideas into your creative process. Find something that you think will look nice and go for it. You create for yourself, and if other people like it, that's a plus. There are many concepts I have drawn up in the past that never left my Lightroom application, but it is because of those failures that I have learned what not to do in the future. Practice isn't what makes perfect, but it does make you a whole lot more experienced.

Figure 8.11

Lastly, the frame itself does not even have to be a common polygon. You can take any silhouette you find that may match the theme of the photo and use it as a negative mask for your image. I used a blurred-out image as the foreground framing for the image and cut it out with an inverse mask of a leaf silhouette.

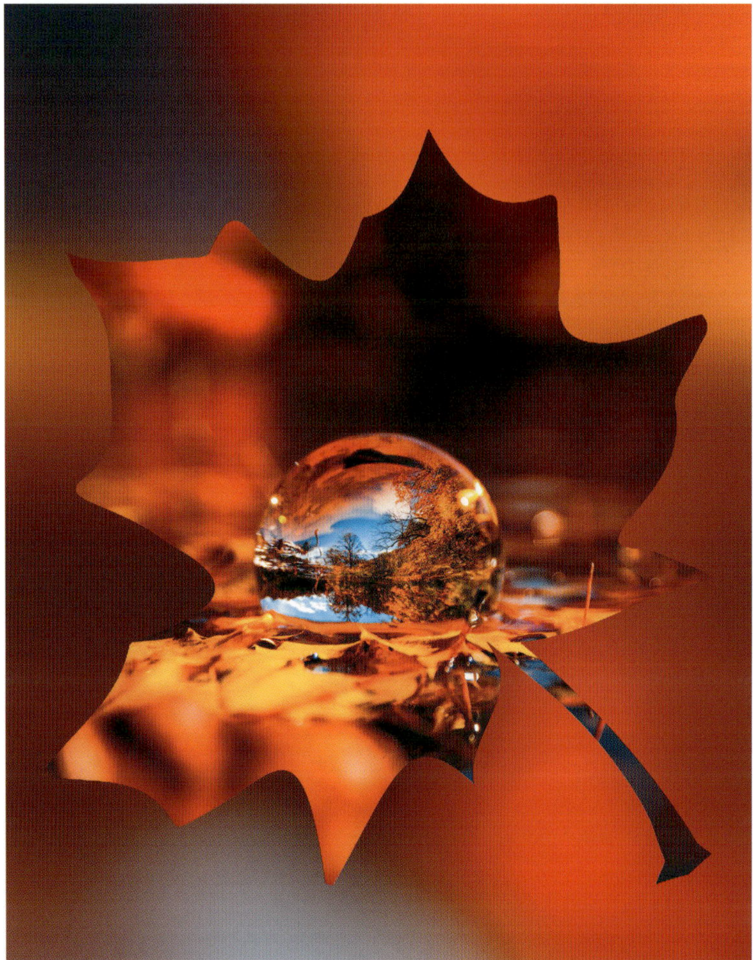

Closing Remarks

The fact that you are reading this means you actually read through the entire book or just skipped all the way to the back for any post-credit scenes. Regardless, I am truly grateful that there are so many of you who share the same passion for photography that I have. I hope you were able to pull inspiration for your future shots from my own creative process, and I wish you the best on your photography journey. As I mentioned earlier, there are no strict rules you must follow to obtain a stunning image. Your intuitive composition should triumph over any rules or theories designed in photography. Basically, capture what you think looks good and study why it looks appealing to you.

The last tip I can leave you with is to let your creativity run wild. Everything I have written prior to this page is just a consolidation of guides, experiences, and information that I would have liked to have known when I started shooting with a lensball. I hope you have gathered all the metaphorical tools you needed from this book to pursue any concepts you want to bring to fruition. If you have any questions or just want to say hi, feel free to contact me on my website or social media pages:

www.marvinlei.com
www.instagram.com/marvinlei

Warm regards,
Marvin Lei

Index